HORSE
NATION

MORE PRAISE FOR
TERESA MARTINO'S WRITING

In a work reminiscent of Joy Adamson's *Born Free*, poet and short story writer Teresa Martino writes about raising a gray wolf and returning it to the wilderness. She reflects thoughtfully on humans living with wild animals....What matters to her are such basic values as loyalty, wildness, and the philosophy of not "bearing" arms. This is an affecting narrative.

—VICKI L. TOY SMITH, *Library Journal*

Teresa Martino speaks eloquently of her own experiences as a human being in a world so alienated from nature, and as one who cannot do other than care deeply for those in her care. Martino's books are highly recommended for everyone who appreciates and honors animals.

—RITA REYNOLDS, *la Joie Journal*

Ms. Martino's prose is poetry, her poetry is magic, her art is native, simplistic, yet simplicity is the most difficult to achieve in communications. She speaks of ancestors, spirits, of heaven and earth, emotions and feelings, not easy revelations.

—DEZSOE STEVE NAGY, *The Latham Letter*

The Wolf, the Woman, the Wilderness is a beautiful, unusual book, one we can all relate to and learn from. There are many who would not choose the life Teresa Martino has chosen, but in all of us there is still some innate strain of "wildness," a yearning for a return to nature.

—VIRGINIA SINK, *The Oklahoma Tribune*

The author's prose is poetic, a blend of beauty and straight-arrow honesty, laced with the wisdom and humor that spring from uncluttered love. Parts of Martino's writing are hilarious, others bring tears, but the greatest gift is the rediscovery of connectedness to the wilderness, to all creatures, to ourselves.

—*Light of Consciousness*

A must read for horse lovers. In simple, compelling language, T. Martino tells tales of her thirty-five-year love affair with horses.

—*Flying Changes Magazine*

HORSE NATION

TRUE STORIES ABOUT HORSES AND PEOPLE

TERESA TSIMMU MARTINO

NEWSAGE PRESS
TROUTDALE, OREGON

HORSE NATION

NewSage Press
PO Box 607
Troutdale, OR 97060-0607
503-695-2211
www.newsagepress.com

Illustrations by Teresa Martino
Cover and Book Design by Sherry Wachter
Printed in the United States on recycled paper

Distributed in the United States and Canada by
Publishers Group West 800-788-3123

NewSage Press Second Edition. First Edition published by NewSage Press in 1999 as *Dancer on the Grass* (ISBN 0-939165-32-5)

Library of Congress cataloging-in-Publication Data

Martino, Teresa.
Horse nation : true stories of horses and people / by Teresa Tsimmu Martino.— 2nd ed.
    p. cm.
Rev. ed. of: Dancer on the grass. 1999.
ISBN 0-939165-51-1
1. Horses—Anecdotes. 2. Horsemen and horsewomen—Anecdotes. 3. Martino, Teresa. I. Martino, Teresa. Dancer on the grass. II. Title.
SF301.M324 2004
636.1—dc22
                                                              2004018144

1 2 3 4 5 6 7 8 9 10

For Pop,
Stoat, Babe, and Bean.

ACKNOWLEDGMENTS

I would like to thank my family for their
understanding and love.

Thank you to my editor and publisher, Maureen R. Michelson,
for all her hard work, dedication and love. And to NewSage
Press for its commitment to my work. A special "thank you"
to Sherry Wachter, for her design work, and to Tracy Smith,
for her attention to editorial detail.

Mary Alice Kier, Thanks! Your wisdom is priceless.

My friends out in Blackfeet country! *Oki! Haway, Wahzhazhe!*

I am grateful to the folks at Sound Food Restaurant for coffee,
love, the table, and electricity!

And thank you Wolftown, the people,
the wolves and the horses!
I'll never run out of stories to tell. You see,
anything is possible....

Thanks, Wire Artist, for belief in the Bohemian.
Thanks Pop! See ya! We will go riding!

CONTENTS

The Song the Stallion Sang
to Black Elk in His Dream

my horses prancing they are coming
my horses neighing they are coming
prancing they are coming
all over the universe they come
they will dance; may you behold them
a horse nation they will dance
may you behold them

—*Black Elk Speaks*

HORSE

NATION

A Kinship with Horses

I met my first horse when I could barely walk. At two years of age, I stumbled into a pasture, drawn to the wonder of a tall, yellow stallion. He stood patiently as I gripped his legs and pulled myself upright. That was my first gift from a horse—support. A few minutes later my relieved parents found me. From that moment forward it was no surprise to them that my life turned into a career with the four-legged spirits who grace the grass.

For more than forty years now I have watched the horses with passion. Horses are my family—sisters and brothers. They are also my teachers and healers. With their mystery and magic, the horses have taught me the speech that transcends verbal language. The horses have shown me spirit and family and leadership. Through the grace of horses I can go back to the time my native ancestors spoke of—when the animals could speak. My father once said, "You want to know what is around you? Ask the horses."

When I was young, my father, Pop, taught me to care for my horses before I cared for myself. He said, "They will always honor you through their work if you do this." He was right. For all of my adult working life, the horses have fed me and kept me free.

Horses run in people's blood, bred into them like spirals of DNA. The sweat of horses and the drumming of their hooves gather horse lovers together like a tribe. This love will keep horse people from buying food for themselves in order to feed their horses first.

This much I know is true: Horse people are like the little trotting sheep dogs bred for years to care for the lambs, or like the children in India who give food to the sacred cattle. This is the way it has been done since the beginning of the partnership between horses and humans. We are happy when working horses, ignoring cold and mud and danger. This is our life; there is no other. The horses know this and they watch us carefully.

The equines are the demi-gods who gave humans power. Their leaping strength, along with alert eyes and swift muscles, allowed humans to be four-legged and gallop across great expanses of land, carrying our spirits. Long before recorded history the horse and human learned how to be molded into one—whether it was the mythic Greek centaur or the Native warrior and pony.

The horses know they are special. Their patient faces are comfortable as they watch us move about busily tending to their needs. They look at us with sweet sympathy, but they know they deserve this care. They know their comfort comes before ours.

The paradox of horses is that they do not have to carry us, but they agree to do so. The horses give their consent and bring a grounding that humanity craves. They also carry the power of wildness that graciously allows us to fly above the land.

I have often wondered, *Did humans really domesticate the horses or did we just form a partnership?* Cooperation is how all life survives. Domestication is a process that works both ways. I believe the horses gentled and tamed humans as well. Humans were once the great hunters of horses but now we serve horses as if they are members of our family. Horses and humans have grown up together. Civilization would be different if it were not for our partnership with horses.

One spring morning, more than forty years after I met my first horse, I was teaching bright faced students the same wisdom and love of horses Pop had given to me. My assistant, Summer, held a colt's head loosely as I stood next to the young horse and leaned into him to tell him with my body what was coming next. Summer was seventeen, the same age I was when I turned professional. "Work with your body," I told Summer. "Listen with it. Your body will tell you if the colt is ready for the next step."

The colt stood calmly, listening to my voice, watching me with soft accepting eyes, feeling my trust of him through my body. Summer continued to hold his head lightly. "You will feel it in your stomach if it is wrong," I continued. "The colt sets the pace for learning. He'll tell your body." Summer nodded sagely. The colt had never been ridden. He gave me his consent and stood quietly, ready for me to get on him.

This young horse and I were starting something that has been done over and over, ever since someone watched the wild herds thunder across plains and imagination. I have worked with more than seven hundred horses over my career and this was the forty-third colt I had started. I have never had a colt buck when I've gotten on. Always, I have asked, and they have given me their consent.

I held up my good leg, the other one weak from repeated injuries. Summer caught it and legged me up the colt's brown shoulder to his warm, bare back. As I stretched across the colt, I wondered, *Who is training whom?*

Feeling the warm body of the three-year-old colt, I imagined how the relationship between horse and human began. Humans and horses have been together for at least five thousand years. Early humans dreamed of horses and painted their images on cave walls in flickering fire light.

Perhaps someone got an idea and thought: *Maybe it would be possible to become horse-like by getting on a horse's back.* I imagine someone found an orphan foal. Maybe hunters killed a mare with a foal and then saw their own human children reflected in the foal's eyes. And in the mare's blood they saw their own fate. Early humans understood that the land gives generously but it also takes back. Hunters knew that one day they would lie as still as their prey. Perhaps the ancestors felt a responsibility for the foal and made a commitment, a promise. Then maybe some child playing with the baby horse climbed on the colt's back and called out to Mom and Dad, "Look! Look!"

Once the horse and human accepted and trusted one another enough to ride together, the human became as swift as the elk and had the senses of an antelope. Suddenly, distances opened up for humanity. They could pursue game like a lion or a wolf. The horses allowed us to become a four-legged animal, a spiritual and bodily transformation into the creature we admired.

Perhaps something about being human with our rational thought and our anguish at the impermanence of life left us lonely. Humanity needed companions with better senses and no long thoughts that dwelt on death. The old people once told me, "The horse and dog are our partners—they came in from the wild to share our lives and ease our fears."

On that spring morning with the colt I noticed the sun coming back after the short days of winter. The light offered hope for the damp, dark Pacific Northwest. A morning chill cut through my blue-leather chaps and my toes were numb in my boots with clinging frozen mud. The strong arm of my student supported me as I looked down at her from the colt's back and asked, "Summer, do you want to be the first to ride him?" The girl's eyes brightened. "Of course!" Then we changed positions.

Other students worked patiently in the barn, learning the commitment needed for caring for the horses. These young people were acolytes as they scrubbed water buckets, cleaned stalls, groomed and fed horses, and rubbed leather with oil and waxy soap.

In the pasture, horses graced the landscape. A brittle breeze plucked long tufts of their winter coat that floated like winged dandelion seeds, coming to rest on sharp, gray-frosted grass. That morning their blooming coats were a bouquet of color—bay, dun, black, chestnut, rust, dapple-gray.

Stallions, mares, geldings, and foals—they are the family of horse. Stars on faces, pearly socks on legs, whorls in hair—all are signs of wisdom or luck. Special horses carry birthmarks on their necks or shoulders, like thumb prints. Pop pointed out these marks to me when I was only four years old. With a hushed voice that hinted of mystery, of sacred things, Pop whispered, "The horses are blessed, chosen by God."

Teresa and Babe

My First Horse

Tradition is a big thing for horse people. Students inherit their teachers' traditions. The classical traditions were only written down a couple of hundred years ago. Most knowledge has been passed down from generation to generation, from teacher to student. My students inherit from me generations of horse work, knowledge gleaned carefully since the beginning of the partnership.

Often my thoughts drift back to my father, who was my first teacher along with my equine teachers, the first horses who led me down this life path. When I was four years old Pop helped me pick my first horse. A tall, bronze-skinned man, Pop carried me through the gate of a rustic post-and-rail fence to where a herd of weaned pony foals stood in a field of dandelions and lupines, and sunshine. He set me down among the tall flowers and curious foals. This was my initiation.

"You pick out one for your own, Teresa," Pop declared. I searched the faces that surrounded me in a loose semi-circle of warm earth colors. One pony was smaller than the rest, a sturdy little gray with a saucy face and warm wise eyes. She walked up and nuzzled my hand, sniffed my hair, considered taking a taste of me, then being a mannered pony, decided against it. Placing my hand on her neck, I said, "This one, Pop!" That was my first real horse.

The little gray pony became a confidant, a compatriot, and a companion. I named her Babe and called her B.B. for short. Pop always called her Rusty because she was the color of a rusty gray nail held in sunlight. Babe was only six months old, too young to ride, so we spent our time together in the fields. Babe grazed close beside me, while I stared up at the clouds and listened to her tear at the grass. When Pop came home from work he would help me brush her, and he showed Babe how to tie and lead and pick up her hooves. Teaching Babe to carry me was easy. I would get on her back when she was lying down and she would groan and sigh, but lay there quietly with my child hands clutching at her mane.

Pop didn't really let me work Babe until she was three years old, and I was seven. By then I could ride Babe into the golden hills and shady orchards near my home. My mother would weave my long dark hair in twin braids down my back, then I would pull on old jeans and boots, and join Babe in the fields.

What did we do, Babe and I? What all horses and children have done. Nothing and everything. Time slowed, disappeared while we watched clouds and chased our shadows through tall grass whipped back and forth like sea water. At any given moment Babe's head could jerk up, her ears prick, and nostrils widen. *What is it?* Babe's body asked me. *Brown's dog or a neighbor girl on her thin bay mare?* Together we would watch and wait. Babe gave me the sharp senses that I would later expand in adulthood, and perfect when I hunted with Mckenzie the wolf.

On the hill above our white house, there was a little sign that pointed and read, "A. Martino." Whenever Babe and I would trot by that old white sign, I believed it meant that there was only one family like mine. My father's first name was Andrew. Perhaps that is why now, as an adult, I go by "T. Martino."

For fun I would put up little obstacles for the pony and ride her bareback at a full gallop down the steepest hills, my arms outstretched, shouting, "Watch me Pop! Watch me!" At a young age I learned that on horseback the world changes. Suddenly you can gallop, you can fly. The horse senses rise up to your soul, absorbed through skin and legs pressed tight. The horse gives these things willingly.

Perhaps some people think riding horses is cruel and that my poor pony, Babe, was dumb and shy, and had to put up with me, her master. Oh! But that is not the way it was. For those who move in close to horses, so close they feel the horses' soft breath, they know horses love, need, and want a good partnership. They look for it even in humanity.

Poor Babe wasn't fast. The neighbors' horses could always outrun us in the honor-bound races we held in the tall old orchards. Other friends' horses were bigger and faster, but Babe could jump, climb the steepest trails, and was unafraid of fierce dogs. She let me do all of these things with her without saddle or bridle, and only with her little halter that Pop had made.

Babe was not a pushover though. One time I tried to lead her through a broken fence line and she refused. For more than an hour I pulled on her, coaxed her—anything—but she would not move. Finally, I had to give up and go around. But on the other hand, Babe actually let me dress her up. One time I put ribbons around her feet and one of Pop's shirts on her. God knows whose pants. Her patience was saintly in that respect.

Falling off Babe became a skill I learned over time. She never bucked but I slipped off and collected my share of bruises, cuts, and tears. After a fall, Babe would nose me, concerned, waiting for me to get back on so we could be on our way.

When I fell, Babe would never leave me. I long for those days. It was good to have a loved one wait for me after I had fallen. But I learned, like life, I must get back up!

As Babe and I grew older, Pop taught me how to sit on her back, balanced, and how to use my weight to talk horse language. This is the empathic speech that runs along muscle and skin, the listening look of pricked ears that reads sights like a dictionary and feels thoughts like a psychic. Horse language is not merely telepathic but rather it is as if all bodies were connected and thoughts ran between them.

Pop taught me to put these feelings and emotions into my mind, and my body would interpret them, and then the feelings would run along my muscles and be communicated to the horse. By learning to put my conscious mind in every part of my body, rather than just in my head, I could talk with a horse in incredible ways.

Now, my talk with horses allows me to ask difficult things from them, like cross-country jumping, or being ridden for the first time, or creating intricate dances. Constantly, I test my communication. If it is correct, the horse does what I ask without force.

My days with my first horse still live in my body. The warm sunlight, the dusty spicy smells of summer, the glimmer of lake water dancing, and my bare feet buried deep in Babe's soft, long belly fur. Her head down in knee-high grass, naked except for me, Babe and I shared a horse's life.

Step…graze…chew…chew. Swish the flies. Step… graze…chew…chew. The Greeks saw centaurs, but I know what they really witnessed—the *partnership*.

Divine Sensation

The Greek historian and commander Xenephon described a special experience a rider and horse can have. He identified the feeling of oneness and power that a rider can share with a horse when they understand one another and move together in balance. He called this "the divine sensation."

The day came when I outgrew my first pony. When I was twelve Pop decided that I needed a big horse. Babe would continue to work by pulling a cart. Pop made her a harness out of scraps of leather in the barn and bought a breaking cart. She pulled me happily, her little hooves click clacking down the road.

Sunny was my first full-sized horse. We found her through a classified ad in the newspaper and bought her from people who were moving out of town. Pop loved her conformation, and I was drawn to her unusual color and yellow eyes. Sunny was a thin mare the color of clay, a dun with a silvery mane and tail. A horse of indeterminate background, we bought her for $400. We had no horse trailer so we walked Sunny the seven miles to our home. Wearing my new boots, I had blisters the size of apricots as I limped to her new paddock.

Sunny did not have a playful or expressive personality, not like clever, sweet Babe who whickered at me or stole my cap. Sunny's eyes were hooded from us, her heart and spirit far away. Pop would offer her a pinch of his pipe tobacco, but even this bribe brought no response. This was puzzling to me. I did not yet understand the ways of horses who had been mistreated.

Sunny must have been drugged when we bought her. We thought she was calm and mellow, but the very next day we saw another side of the mare. She was standing peacefully in her paddock when our cowboy neighbor, Dean, hiked over and neatly swung himself into her corral. Dean thought our horsemanship was lacking. After all, what could Pop, an Italian from Brooklyn, know about horses?

He strolled up to Sunny as if he were John Wayne and looked at her appraisingly. He pushed his Stetson back, took a pull on his cigarette and turned away, the smoke trickling out of his mouth. Suddenly, as the cowboy turned, the mare's ears swept back as if they disappeared, and she half reared and charged. The poor cowboy turned and for a split second stared at the mare. Sunny launched herself at him stirring up a great cloud of dust. Dean turned and ran for his life, his boots ringing like bells on the dry, dusty dirt.

Pop and I looked at each other, stunned, then looked back at the incredible scene wondering if the cowboy would make the fence before the pounding hooves. The mare was gaining, her teeth bared, and her eyes blazing serious. If Sunny caught Dean he was dead. With an amazing burst of speed, the cowboy jumped the post and rail like a gazelle without even touching it with his hands. He kept running, not chancing that the mare would jump the fence and finish the job on his property.

Pop then turned to me and said in a matter-of-fact voice, "Sister, this horse will really teach you to ride." I trusted my father but I wondered about this statement. About that time my Italian Grandma Connie came out of the house. She wiped her hands on her apron as she watched Dean run on over the hill. Delighted with the fleeing figure, she declared, "Serves him right. That man watches me through my window!" Then she looked at me, her eyes like raisins, and advised, "Squeeze rocks, it'll make your hands strong so you can hold on to that mare better."

At twelve years old I rec-ognized danger in the eyes of Sunny. When Pop came

Teresa and Sunny

home after work he would work with me and Sunny. Pop taught me on the mare, and the mare taught me in her own way. Sometimes, the cowboy would watch over the fence. The mare would look at him and her ears would go back. Years later I realized the cowboy reminded Sunny of someone who had hurt her.

Sunny was dominant, probably because of the abuse she had suffered. She refused to turn and would often rear and buck if I asked her to go forward. Pop thought she was a little like Grandma Connie. This became a fundamental problem in riding Sunny, but she certainly taught me to control my fear. If I was afraid, I couldn't work with her because she would feel it, smell it, sense it like ice forming on a pond. And once Sunny knew I was fearful she would do nothing for me.

I loved Sunny with her unusual clay color and graceful body like a desert antelope. Her eyes were the strangest I had seen, almost yellow like a wolf. She was not registered with any breed association and Dean commented on her being a scrub horse with no pedigree. So Pop and I found a registry that would take her, the Buckskin Horse Association. When we got her papers, Pop proudly strode out into the field with Sunny and yelled at Dean to come over and look at her beautiful registration. But the mare stared at Dean and whickered strangely. The cowboy waved at Pop but did not attempt to cross the field to see the mare's pedigree. He saw it in her eyes. I think this pleased Pop, and Grandma Connie laughed out right as she watched from the kitchen doorway.

Sunny didn't love me. She didn't even look at me when I came out in the morning to feed her. When I curried her she was indifferent, which always surprised me because grooming is an intensely social act. Most horses cannot resist grooming. Sunny's indifference hurt me deeply because I expected my horse to love me. I couldn't understand why she did not.

After a couple of months working with Sunny I could take her out on the trails and at last, we found something we both loved. Sunny loved to run, and with me on her back we joined the "Our Gang" of the hills. Along with other dusty children and horses, we rode. Every type of horse and child rider challenged us to race. Sunny and I always won. I was a nobody in school—shy, aloof, finding almost no one to talk to or connect with—but on those trails with Sunny I was the *one*.

About one year after we bought Sunny, something changed. One day while I was cleaning Sunny's stall the dun mare looked at me and nickered. Mid-swing with the pitch fork, I stopped, and swung around to look at Sunny. My dark hair fell in my eyes like Sunny's own silvery forelock. We stared at one another. Her strange yellowish eyes gazed at me with love. She whickered again softly, a deep throaty mare sound, unlike a stallion's high-pitched voice. Some thirty years later I can still feel the power of that mare's eyes. Clearly, I see dust motes riding on bright streams of summer sunlight, and in the midst of that curtain of light, the dun mare calls to me. In that moment, Sunny forgave me for being human.

With Sunny I experienced the "the divine sensation," the feeling of oneness and power that you share with the horse when you both understand one another and move together in balance.

One day after working with Pop, Sunny arched her back, gathered her hind legs far under her body, and softened her jaw and expression. I was no longer a dusty child in cutoffs, bareback on an ornery mare. Instead, I was an emperor riding home to admiring millions after saving my country from certain destruction. I was Artemis chasing deer, my bow to shoulder under the ancient moon. I was the Osage girl in the sea of grass. In that glorious moment the mare swung under me with the grace of open water, and with the trust of a puppy. Pop described it as "a collected trot correctly on the frame."

After that first experience of "divine sensation" the floodgates of love opened between Sunny and me. Now Sunny understood our partnership and we began to work as one body. We talked as we rode. Still, we owned no saddle and I had never shown her in competition.

There were few people who witnessed the love that unfolded between Sunny and me. My family knew, especially Pop, and beyond them there was one special friend, Dee Dee. We had known one another since kindergarten, and we often played horse in the playground, imagining ourselves as romantic, brave horse characters who led exciting lives.

Dee Dee admired Sunny and would often watch on the sidelines as Sunny and I worked in the arena. She told me she couldn't ride because she had some strange blood disease that made her weak and thin. Dee Dee had always been furious with her sickness and had told me how she felt so frequently that I began to feel guilty about my own good health. Dee Dee told me she was angry because she would never drive a car, go to Africa, get a job she loved, ride a horse fast and furious.

It is Dee Dee's life, and death when she was only twelve years old, that became a trail marker for me. Often I have thought of Dee Dee, particularly when I have been disappointed and pained about my own life. When I think of all that Dee Dee did not get to experience, and the tremendous pain she felt daily, until the day she died, I am grateful for the fullness of my life. The night after her memorial service I dreamed of Dee Dee in a riding hall. She and I stood still and horses and riders wheeled around us. She told me, "I'm not angry any more Teresa." And I believed her.

Just as the horses were teaching me about the brilliance and exhilaration of life, Dee Dee initiated me into another realm— the impermanence of life and the reality of death. We are always dying, all of us. Back then I was far from that knowledge, but it had brushed my cheek with a cool finger. The precious knowing that life is change.

That winter Sunny developed a terrible abscess, right between her front legs. It was hot and swollen, and Pop could not find an entry hole of a foreign body, maybe from a sliver of wood. Day after day Pop had me foment the abscess with warm, damp towels. Three times a day I stood under Sunny with dripping towels, patiently caring for her. The mare's coat became rough and her weight dropped. Babe stood by us, her little nose just touching Sunny's leg. Mares bond deep, intense about their friendships and loves. I have seen them pine for months over a lost companion. In a herd of horses, the family is mostly female with generally only one stallion. Babe and Sunny loved each other. They called to each other when separated, and greeted each other joyously. The two mares communicated by voice and touch, standing close, content that a friend was near by. Mares are like women.

Finally, the abscess burst and with its draining Sunny got better. We eagerly waited for spring when Sunny would be well and we could ride together. Sunny and I shared a unique partnership, we understood the divine sensation when horse and human are one. There would be more joyful rides for Sunny and me, yet the day would come when life would turn our happiness upside down.

Pop and Dolly

My Teachers,
the Horses and Humans

T hroughout my growing years I witnessed many deaths of people I loved. I wonder if this didn't push my kinship with the horses up a notch—giving me the broken-hearted sympathy that allows me to see the animals as people. Perhaps it was because the people around me who were dying were not afraid. From them I learned the preciousness of life, and to have the courage to live every moment.

The horses and death gave me the courage to cross-country jump, start up colts, and have the bravery to do hard things. People often seek safety, but long ago I decided, *There isn't safety, just life.*

My father was born in Brooklyn, the son of immigrant Italian parents. My Grandpa Natali had trained at a cavalry school in Italy, which was the equivalent of the French cavalry center at Saumur and the Spanish Riding School in Vienna. These European schools taught the old art of equestrian lore, the art of perfecting the combined performance of horse and rider. When Grandpa Natali left his Italian homeland and moved to Brooklyn, he worked as a shipwright and a bricklayer to support his family. This was a far cry from the soft signals between horse and rider.

Grandpa Natali was killed in a car accident. Soon after that Grandma Connie moved the family to Long Island. It was on Long Island that Pop learned his horse skills without his father. He did what all poor kids must do if they love horses and must ride—he shoveled stalls for lessons. Pop learned to jump and do dressage. After World War II, when Pop was twenty-five years old, he bought his first horse, a small chestnut mare. He paid $20 for Dolly.

Pop was wistfully sad when he would tell me about Dolly and how much he loved her. He finally had to sell her because his family needed money. As a child I didn't understand this. I wondered, *How can you sell someone you love?* Years later I would understand that this is the curse of horses—to have a beautiful partner, one you love, and one you have to sell in order to feed your children, or the rest of the barn.

Memories of Pop flow through my life like rivers—sometimes roaring with white rapids, painful with ice, or sweet like slow summer water. He was the type of man who made ordinary things seem incredible. He often had a look of amazement—a wild man, tamed. One of the last things Pop told me before he died was to "stay young," which I interpreted as "keep on wondering." He said fear makes people old. Once he told me that he would like to sell everything and live in a travel trailer by the river rather than live the normal way.

As my teacher, the most important gift Pop gave me was an appreciation for and a knowledge of the classical art of riding. When I was twelve he gave me the book, *The Complete Training of Horse and Rider* by Alios Podhajsky. This was among the first written accounts of the oral tradition from the Spanish Riding School of Vienna. It is an old style of work in which the rider uses no force. It takes years to find the perfect balance between horse and rider.

After many years the horse and rider experience a bonding that feels as if they are one body, not two. Horses I have raised and started under saddle feel as if my own spirit rests inside them, and their horse spirit looks at the world through my eyes. Pop also taught me some horses, like people, only reach a certain point athletically. A wise teacher of horses recognizes this and stops, and lets the horse be where he or she can succeed.

Pop said something that I still tell my students forty years later. "Tell the horses what you are doing. Talk to the horses, tell them your mind. You can't lie to horses." When I am having problems, I go about my barn chores telling the horses what is wrong. They listen with long faces and bright eyes and pricked ears. After that, the horses and I are kinder with one another.

As a freshman in high school I was restless, longing for the openness of the outdoors and the lessons nature wanted to teach me. In the classroom I drew horses and wondered why teachers taught subjects they didn't love. Daily, I watched the clock, waiting to be free. When I got home I would ride Sunny in the fields and watch wildlife from her back. It was there that I watched people's attitudes about wild animals. The coyotes and rattlesnakes who lived around us were hated by most of the ranchers, but I loved to watch the wild.

A few months after my friend Dee Dee died, death visited again. One night at supper, Pop answered the phone. A few minutes later, he hung up, stood in the kitchen awhile and stared out at the towering pepper trees. When he came back to the dining room, he bent his head down to his plate, and began to weep openly. My mother, brother, and I sat there shocked. Grandma Connie was dead from a massive coronary.

At Grandma Connie's funeral I looked at her soft face and thought of her stories of the days when there were no cars. Once she fought with a man who was beating his tired old cart horse to force it up a hill. Grandma Connie fought the man physically and won. She hit him with a broom.

Within a year after the death of his mother, Pop seemed restless. He had his first heart attack when he was forty-two. The day it happened Mom picked me up at school. We drove to the hospital in almost complete silence. I understood by her face and body that Pop was sick. When he came home he was different—weaker and frightened. Then one afternoon he had another episode and I was sent down the hill to wait for the ambulance by the sign that read, "A. Martino."

When the ambulance attendants loaded Pop up, my mother and I got in the back with him for the ride to the hospital. Pop's hand, gray and trembling, reached out. My mother said in a small, pathetic, hopeless way, "Andy, what do you want?"

Pop looked around confused, then replied, "I want you to hold my hand." Mom held his hand and I held his arm. We were too scared and shocked to cry. Even now that pain is held in my belly like a stone. At thirteen years old, I knew that I would lose my best and dearest friend early, and spend many years missing him. Nothing is permanent. It took me years to learn that there is beauty in the ephemeral.

Months later, after Pop recovered, he decided to move the family north to a little valley in the coastal mountains. Before he died, he wanted to do what he and his brothers had come to California to do—buy a ranch. So Pop bought land with my mother's misgivings. We moved from the white house on the hill where I was raised, and where I knew every rock and tree. We drove eight hours away, far from the sign that read "A. Martino."

I still dream of that house—how the morning light came into my room through the homemade curtains with the blue-green balloon pattern. I remember the shapes of the doors and the cool feel of the brass doorknobs; and the huge pepper tree that leaned against the roof in winter storms. If places can remember, that place remembers me. The rooms remember Granny and Grandma Connie at Christmas. They remember Dee Dee's laugh and my mother's warm hugs. The walls remember my father and his dreams for his family in the sunny land of California.

The move was long, and the work considerable. We had to build a house and a barn. Temporarily, there was a little shed for Babe and Sunny and a small paddock. The house took about six months to build and was done in the fall. Granny and Grandpa, my mother's parents, came and helped paint our house.

My mother's parents were originally from Arkansas, and had native blood, Osage. Grandpa's love was for mules, and he and Pop frequently argued the merits of horses and mules. Grandpa believed mules were far more intelligent than horses. Pop declared that mules had no honor. I always wondered about horse honor. *What was that?* Now I think, *It must be that horses will attempt the impossible for you, while mules will think you are foolish and quit.*

Granny was an Ozark farm girl who loved to talk about the various plow horses she had known when she was young. And how all ten of her brothers and sisters would ride them down to White River to swim. All my life, Grandpa and Granny lived close by. My mother and Granny were like sisters.

One afternoon Granny and I ran along the river by our house. Our hair streamed out and our breath came fast. Granny stopped once and a butterfly, caught up in our breeze, landed on her. With the wonder of a girl, Granny said, "Look! Look Teresa

Ann!" Standing by the bright running water, her red hair bristled the same color as the butterfly's wings. Granny stood still with the symbol of change sitting on her breast. Later, Mom would tell me that Granny was dying of cancer.

One year after building our house, the barn, and the fences, Pop's doctor told him to sell the ranch, live quietly, and he might have another year of life. Pop's arteries were blocked, and inoperable. So we moved back to our old community where my mother could be close to Granny.

We did not get the house of my childhood back, or land enough for our horses. We lived in a motel for months while we tried to find a house. We gave Babe to a family friend, and asked a close neighbor to sell Sunny for us. My only request was that the new owner call me if Sunny was ever for sale again. Our family finances were so shaky the future was uncertain. We even had to give away one dog and some of our cats.

Grandpa's brother Quincy died and soon after his wife, Aunt Ottie. We buried them in the cemetery below Mt. Diablo where Granny and Pop would eventually lie, too. Granny continued to waste away with the cancer and the treatments. Her youngest brother, Wayland, came to California to visit her. He had never been out of the mountains of Arkansas, had never been on a bus, and had never seen the ocean. But he came out to say good-bye to his sister. He and Granny talked of old times, and they smiled and laughed as if she were merely going off to the desert to hike and look at cactuses. The two of them acted as if they would meet again in their old hometown of War Eagle and go swimming.

Uncle Wayland and I hit it off immediately. In him I saw wildness. He could drink whiskey like water and chewed tobacco, though he was careful to spit it outside. He laughed like a boy when the sea water waves touched his bare feet for the first time, his overalls rolled up past his knees. When he went back to Arkansas, he called me from the one little store where there was a pay phone, promising, "I'll send you a mule, or a barefoot boy!"

After Granny died it was not long before Uncle Wayland died. The doctors had told him his liver was bad from drinking. He laughed, left the hospital, got into his old red pickup truck, and drove off. He died in a car accident on the way home.

Their matter-of-factness about dying gave me courage. Granny even told Mom how she wished to be buried, what dress she wanted to wear, who she wanted to attend her wake and funeral, and who would be allowed to see her dead body. This I witnessed. Granny gave me her carved wooden mules that had come from a mountain man in Arkansas, and the necklace she had worn when she married. One night, she whispered to me, "I will come back as a panther." Much later when I saw mountain lions, I looked closely into their eyes to see if Granny was there.

After every one of these people died, I dreamed of them— vivid dreams in which they came back to tell me they were okay. Granny came to me in her long, black-and-white party dress, the one she had worn for her twenty-fifth wedding anniversary. In the dream, I laid my head on her knees and she stroked the back of my head saying, "I've got to go away now, but it will be all right."

Years later my memory still shrinks at this, Granny dead and Pop so sick. Pop taught me what to do if he had a heart attack. I learned CPR early. How frightened my mother was! Our finances grew scarce with mounting doctor bills, and Pop not able to work. He collected disability and I got some Social

Security money, which I signed over to the family every month. Mom got me a part-time job with a veterinarian and I contributed money to the family.

My mother and father tried to hide the worst, their anger with a situation that would not be all right. But they were falling down a hole with no rope, no light, no hope. Now, I dreamed strange ugly dreams. For most of my life I had fed horses, but in these dreams the horses were starving because I hadn't fed them. I would wake with a start and realize, once again, our horses were gone.

High school was almost impossible. At seventeen years old I was too busy with life learning about mortality. I had to figure out how to survive in the haze of Pop's illness and Granny's cancer. I often wondered, *How can I concentrate on schoolwork that seems meaningless?*

My spirit took on a darkness, a color dim and hidden under fallen leaves. I grew to hate hospitals where Pop often slept. And I began to kiss him good night every time knowing that one day he would be gone. Pop had been my protector, my guardian, the father who wished to "give me away" one day at my wedding. He was the friend I shared horses with, and he was dying and there was nothing anyone could do. Anger and compassion filled me up simultaneously.

Pop had amber eyes and blue-black hair, as curly as a lamb's. When I was a child I had seen a movie about pirates, and after that I thought Pop looked like a pirate. One time, near the end of his life, Pop asked me, "I wonder why you want to spend time with me, Sister, I'm old and sick." I looked at him and said, "Pop you're like Errol Flynn in *Robin Hood.* You are my hero." Pop was silent. Then he grabbed my hand tightly, held on, and kept walking, staring straight ahead.

Through all of this I still rode horses. Like Pop had done when he was young, I shoveled stalls for riding lessons. Soon I was exercising horses for the trainers. The year before Pop died I had the opportunity to train in England for my preliminary instructor's certificate offered by the British Horse Society.

Pop and Mom were supportive, excited by the promise of my life, and they helped all they could. Sitting in the airport before I left for England, Pop said, "I could go with you, I got my passport."

I shook my head and smiled. "Pop, I've got to do this by myself. I'll be back in four months." I think Pop knew that he was very close to the dark and that he might not ever see me again. Or perhaps he was simply afraid to see his daughter go to Britain alone.

England was the adventure that gave me time to escape from the pain at home. Pop and Mom wrote long letters often. In fact, no one else at the school got so many letters and I was always asked to share Pop's humorous notes before dinner. He wrote his letters in all different colors and with weird little drawings and silly poems. He said that he remembered what it was like being away from home, and how important it was to get letters. Years later, I still keep these letters with me.

After completing my instructor's certificate program, I was asked to stay on in England and work, but one gray day the phone rang. It was Pop. "Come home," was all he quietly said and I asked no questions. I flew back in September after passing all my exams at the British Horse Society. Pop would be dead by January.

When I returned home, Pop wanted to go fly-fishing, but he was too sick. So, we inflated a yellow raft, placed it in a swimming pool, and floated. Pop threw his fly line. When it got caught in the trees, I would climb out of the swaying raft and untangle it for him. Then Pop would row slowly around the pool, amazement still lighting his face, remembering the rivers.

One day I took a long drive to the ranch we had built in the northern coastal mountains. I was gathering memories, my strength for an uncertain future. My heart still ached losing Babe, and having to sell Sunny for money. In a field strung with wire, I saw a skinny, rough-coated dun mare. I called to her, but she never looked up. She stood hip cocked, sightlessly staring at the ground. The mare was Sunny. Her fight was over and her spirit now hid in a slave's body. The girl who had bought Sunny had seemed so nice. What had happened? Why did she sell the mare without calling me as she had agreed? Or was she the one who had let the mare come to this?

When I told my family, Pop looked at me with the same tired inward stare that Sunny had given me. He could not help me save her. Later, going back to the field, the dun mare was gone. I never saw Sunny again. However, Babe was still with our friends, teaching their girls what she had taught me. She would stay with this family and live until her late teens. When she died, they buried her on their farm in an honored place.

Two weeks before Pop died, we did two things together. We looked at colts and we looked at a small farm for sale. Pop smiled and laughed that day but he walked slowly. While I rode a colt, he offered advice, occasionally dreaming out loud. "We'll buy a farm where you can ride and teach," he said. "And we'll buy a fabulous colt who will win everything in sight." Perhaps Pop felt bad deep down that he would die not able to help me live and work.

Then he was gone. He died outside in the sun. Pop fell like the Little Prince—softly, gently. The painless arrows of Apollo had hit him, those special arrows that the ancient

Greeks believed were reserved for the good people. He fell and was gone. After that, I never dreamed of Pop. Instead, I dreamed of horses.

Long ago, I was richer than any billionaire. My living money ran over the grass. My bank was my skill with the long rope and an ability to balance on a horse without thinking.

Now, those memories are like dreams. Babe is dust, green grass, and earth—but she is still in me. At night in dark dreams I still see her, feel her, hear her hooves in creek water, and click-clacking on the hard trail. Clumps of her rusty-gray fur still stick to me.

My family members who have died are somewhere. Wayland swims in the White River with flashing strong strokes. Grandma Connie writes love poetry about horses and strength. Granny stalks the deer trails as the gray panther of the hills.

Babe, and Sunny, and Pop, started me on this trail. Babe taught me gentleness and strength of character. Sunny taught me how to win over hatred with love. Pop gave me wings. His horse blood gallops through my body, and my heart beats to the rhythm of hoof beats. I know in the spirit world Pop rides Dolly and looks for me. This thought keeps him alive.

Often I light candles for my family—all priests and priestesses of my horse temple, brothers and sisters of my horse nation. My silent prayer: *Let me always ride horseback!* It means more than life to run and jump and be with horses. The nomad in me calls out to the dusty plains and the soft whickers of horses. Every day a blessing stands in my fields and watches me.

Now, my life work is to pass on these gifts to other people. To share how glorious it feels to run on horseback, wind in your face. To live without fear of dying!

To the One
Who Gave Me Horses

Your footsteps fade
into the long grass
The sky is darkened.

We hear your call no more.

The stars turn from behind
the clouds.
The sun comes.
We remember
the glance, the hand's caress,
the dear face and noble mind.

I had seen the falcon.
He sped across the sky,
light over his wings.
He rode the wind.

The sun and moon
have turned many times
and my spirit doesn't cry your name.

I understand you rode the wind
as the falcon.
I rode the earth
with the horses.

The horses, Father, were your
gift of life to me.
I know now
hey, we'll meet again.
On the narrow trail,
the trail following
the sunset path.

Fallen

As I dismounted the colt spooked a foolish colty spook. I was already half way out of the saddle so his twirling spin threw me off his back. I slammed into a fence post.

The impact forced the air out of my lungs and I crumpled to the ground gasping. Slowly, I got back on my feet, but the pain on my left side felt like large jagged glass digging deep. I staggered out of the ring and sat on the grass. The colt's concerned owner, Tracy, shouted across the ring, "Are you all right?"

"Oh yes…I'm…wind knocked out of me, that's all." But something was wrong; my body felt strange. Suddenly, moments stretched out on the cool breeze and I slipped into unconsciousness. I lay in the tall grass dreaming as my body went into shock. In my unconscious reality, I saw a familiar figure—it was Harry, the short Englishman. He stood before me in his shiny black boots and tweed coat. Then he knelt in the frosty, sharp, fall grass, and chided me: "God! Martino! That was a stupid fall! Didn't you hear me say, 'Watch him?'" In dream time I slowly answered, "Oh, yeah. Sorry sir."

Then consciousness woke me. In front of my nose, I noticed the grass and the little cold spiders clinging to it. Harry was gone. I felt no pain, only a woozy sweet lightness. *Where am I?* I wondered. *What had happened?* I couldn't remember. Looking up I saw Tracy standing over me. Then I remembered. *Oh! The colt! I had fallen.*

"Not again! Sorry Harry!" I said out loud to my dream teacher. Lying there, I smiled. I always think of Harry when I fall.

Before long there were sirens, volunteer firefighters, and even a tired sheriff. They strapped me tightly to a backboard. I knew I had broken ribs, familiar with that sharp ringing stab of pain. Possibly I was bleeding internally. As the ambulance headed for the hospital, I watched the sunset melt into Puget Sound and turn the snow-covered Olympic Mountains reddish pink like salmon flesh. The bumps in the dirt road jabbed at my broken body.

Smiling, I asked Stan the paramedic, "Would you want to die doing something you love?" Stan said nothing. He was monitoring my blood pressure.

"Uh oh!" mumbled Stan, watching my blood pressure drop. "Uh oh?" I weakly joked. "Stan, that's pretty alarming bedside manner."

At the hospital three friends sat with me as the surgeon explained my medical situation. They determined that a number of my ribs had been broken, but it was hard to tell exactly the number since I had broken so many before. My spleen was bruised and leaking blood into the sack that surrounded it. "We may have to remove your spleen if it doesn't seal," explained the doctor. "Try not to remove my spleen, okay?" I whispered, feeling out of breath. The doctor looked at me with a serious granite face. "If you move around you could die."

For four days I lay in intensive care, my body a knot of immense pain. I worried about the wolves and the horses. My world was filled with suffering and I could only view it from moment to moment. Often I considered taking a lot of the pain killers and then sleeping free of this agony. But only when I felt I could bear it no longer did I take the drugs the nurses offered.

Riders get hurt. How many friends have I had who limped, walked stiffly, or ended up paralyzed because of injuries? There were many. Two friends broke their necks, and one ended up a quadriplegic. One accident happened right in front of me while we were running steeplechase. Other friends have broken their backs. Two of my friends, both professional riders, had been killed while cross-country jumping. Many times I have asked myself, *What is it that makes us risk this?*

Horses and injuries are like the shadow of war. Equestrian eventing is a sport that comes out of the traditions of the cavalry, different than the quiet art of dressage or the sweetness of walking a mountain trail. Eventing comes from the idea that a soldier was given a message and he had to run cross-country to deliver it to his commander. Accomplishing this feat under the threat of death was a challenge and a thrill that still echoes through modern cross-country horse events.

For me, this dangerous risk-taking was a way back into wilderness where the antelope runs from the wolf in fear and joy. *Did I want to go back to the wild?* I asked myself. There are other sports that are dangerous, but for me galloping horses cross-country gives the electric feel of the elk running.

After the fourth day the doctors let me go home with the grave warning that just one jounce and I could start bleeding again. For the next twelve weeks I had to lie in my dusty trailer healing. My community came and went, bringing me food, company, and help with my wolf rescues. As I watched the shy wolves slink in and out through the cold of my open trailer door, day after day, I thought of many things. I thought of Harry, and of falling.

Harold Fitzwalter was the managing instructor at The Vale Equestrian Center in England. He was a small man with ginger-colored hair and stern gray eyes. He carried himself with the demeanor of an old-time British colonel, yet he was only twenty-four. Harry did not walk, he marched.

When we first met, he strode across the main yard with his shiny black boots clacking on the cobblestones. He gripped my sweaty palm as tightly as a gun handle and gave me a grim smooth handshake. "How do you do. Your quarters are over there—the grooms' quarters over the main barn." Then he added, "You look a sight! Go clean up and come to tea." His voice was brusque, but the English accent made him sound rather charming. Harry was unlike anyone I had ever met. Tough, cool, and very British.

I had just arrived in England, an eager nineteen-year-old student training for my preliminary instructor's certificate. There were ten students attending the training: Three from the United States, two from Italy, one from Sweden, one from Ireland, and three from England. We had been accepted to train at the toughest school in Britain. Each student had been carefully selected because The Vale had a 100 percent pass rate on the British Horse Society tests. If there was a chance a student would not pass the training in four months, The Vale didn't want that person. One of my coaches in America had trained at The Vale and she had written my letter of introduction and recommendation.

At The Vale we studied every aspect of horse work, including riding, jumping, stable management, and veterinary care. We were trained to be pro. The work was hard. We often put in fifteen-hour days with one day off a week to do our laundry. Given this kind of regimen, it did not take long for the ten of us to become friends.

Ian, the Irish student, and I quickly became buddies. He had a cheerful sense of humor. With his light brown hair and slender good looks he resembled an elf king from a Tolkien novel. We were yard mates and took care of four horses together.

After work Ian and I were pranksters, stealing biscuits from the kitchen for midnight snacks. We were as full of high spirits as the colts we rode. One time we trapped a weak instructor and threw him into the water jump. For that stunt, Harry gave us extra work detail as punishment, shoveling manure out of fields.

Before long, Harry became the bane of my life. I in turn was chaos to him, the dark at the window. He told me I was "undisciplined, as awkward as an animated banana, and I had hands like a blacksmith." We had declared war on each other.

The Vale was based on many years of tradition and strict discipline. The tack shone and the horses gleamed. The cobblestones in the main yard were spotless, not one piece of chaff or straw ever rested upon them for long. The stalls were as sanitary as a hospital.

Harry was our zealous commandant. We braided the horses' manes every morning and Harry would inspect our work with a frowning face. My braids frequently got pulled out. I was always late for breakfast because I was constantly redoing braids. I was convinced Harry hated me. At lecture he asked me tough questions such as, "Martino, what is the protein percentage of whole oats?"

Some of these questions I couldn't answer. I had to respond bluntly, "I don't know, sir." Then Harry would look as severe as possible, and deliver his harsh retorts. "You don't know?

Do you know how to read? Do they read in California, you rotten urchin?"

Ian always laughed when I got into trouble and then he would get into hot water himself. "Ian, if you laugh you will be cleaning tack till half nine tonight," Harry would growl at him.

At some point during the four-month training, everyone fell, usually when they were jumping. When students fell they had to put money in the "team jar," a pound note to be donated to the British Olympic Team.

About half way through the course everyone had fallen but me. I had my share of close calls, but Pop's way of training me to ride without a saddle and my horse Sunny's hot ways had helped me develop the seat of a professional.

Harry soon noticed that I had not yet fallen. This bothered him. One morning he walked up to me after breakfast, and like a king he looked me up and down to see if my clothes, hair, or boots were out of place. I had taken particular care that morning. I was spit shined and ready for him. "Martino, I want you to jump Bushman cross-country today," commanded Harry. My eyebrows rose. Bushman was easily the hottest horse at the school. A tall chestnut horse with long legs and an elegant neck, Bushman was a fierce four-year old. Ian described this horse as "a bucking bloody fool."

"Uh, Bushman?" I asked in disbelief. "He has been stalled for two days. Don't you want to hack him quietly in the fields today?"

Harry smiled through his mustache. "Are you afraid, Martino? Think you can't sit him? You smug Americans! Take him out!" Then turning on immaculate boots, Harry strode away.

Ian walked up to me. "Aye, well, tough luck! I'll say a rosary for you T." Ian put a comforting hand on my shoulder.

"Thanks Irish," I muttered, and slumped off to saddle up for doomsday.

Harry's smile was mean as he faced the line of students. He checked our tack for cleanliness, our braids for neatness, our boots for shine. He sent one student back to rebraid. Then the rest were sent out to warm up for cross-country school. As I quietly passed by, Harry clapped Bushman on the rump and sneered, "Let's see how good you are, California." Bushman jumped and bucked in response but I had a good hold on the horse.

Bushman was as high as a kite that morning having been locked in his box stall for two days. I wondered, *God! Did Harry do that on purpose?* At first, I rode Bushman carefully and tried to get him to relax, but whenever another horse went by us in the grassy fields Bushman would buck and rear.

As I rode Bushman it was obvious that I was nowhere close to falling off. Harry's face darkened. After warm-up, we students formed a line and were sent off to work the downhill cross-country course. This course was preliminary sized but it was big enough for a green horse like Bushman. Harry instructed me to go last. While waiting I realized Harry wanted Bushman to be excited by all the other horses going before us. By the time our turn came my belly was tight but I was determined not to fall.

When we started out, Bushman took hold of the bridle and pulled hard. I half halted, released, and talked soothingly to him. We jumped up the big bank, did a 90-degree turn and came bucking down the hill to the big drop. At the last second I got Bushman's head up so he would realize what we were jumping. After the drop was a line of fences in combination with a big ditch under the second element and then up a hill to another big log pile. By that time I was frantically trying to slow Bushman down. We came to level ground, splashed into the water jump, and sprang forward to breeze past the group who stood and watched.

Harry was smiling like a devil. "Ah, very good Martino," he slyly offered as I pulled Bushman up to him. "Very impressive. Now, please do the coffin with no hands. Knot your reins."

"No hands?" I asked, stunned by his request. "Uh, Bush will run away."

"Scared to do it?" Harry smiled grimly.

"No," I responded, determined not to let him win this battle.

Now it was my turn to get serious. I glared at Harry with the fierceness of a hawk. Then Harry announced, "You may gather up your reins when you get out the other side."

My fellow students held a collective breath. I glanced at Ian. He was shaking his head. "Don't do it, T!" he whispered. "You'll get killed. That old bastard! He can't make you do it."

Harry walked up between us and looked into my eyes. Harry whispered savagely, "Oh, Daddy would think you could do it. Martino, you live in Walt Disneyland. Let's see what you are made of my girl." Then he turned to Ian: "Mr. Murphy, no stirrups, around the whole course posting trot, go." Ian glared at him, then folded the stirrups neatly over his horse's neck and grimly headed out.

I stroked Bushman's neck. Pop had always believed in my ability to ride, not like Harry who seemed determined to get me killed. In one of Pop's letters he wrote, "I know you are feeling nervous about passing your exams. Believe in yourself, Teresa. Say every day, 'I'm getting better and better in my ability as a horsewoman.' I believe in you!"

Pop's daily letters had become popular group reading material at dinner. Harry had always ridiculed my father's encouraging letters as "Walt Disneyland." He also criticized my inability to "let go of my family and grow up." I didn't understand Harry's anger at the simple love Pop and I shared.

I glanced at the rare cloudless Somerset sky, determined. Harry smiled again then growled low, "You're off this time." I knew I had one chance. If Bushman jumped the fences fast he might not put his head down. Harry hadn't said jump the whole course without reins.

I picked Bushman up and we galloped off. The first part of the course was again a battle of bucking and trying to keep the strong-willed horse's head up. Then came the big drop fence to the coffin combination. I lightened my reins to butter. That simple test made Bushman think about his own balance rather than fighting me. In that moment, I learned one of the most important things in riding and life: *Sometimes letting go is better.*

Then we were at the coffin. I felt the wild rush of confidence and instead of grabbing mane and dropping reins, I stuck both my arms out like an airplane and flew through. Luckily, Bushman, though wild, was honest. He went straight at his jumps. But after the last element his head went down and I made a wild swoop for the reins and missed. He bucked one time, head down, heels high. I was flung far up his neck. Dimly I could hear Harry laughing.

Bushman then did something amazing. The hot-blooded chestnut stopped. I was on his neck clinging with arms and legs sideways. If Bush had sneezed, I would have fallen off, but the tall gelding just stood there. Perhaps he was surprised at me hanging off his neck.

The group was silent except for Harry laughing so loudly I thought he would fall down. My face was hot with blood and shame. *Why was this man torturing me?* I wondered as I considered what to do next.

From beyond the group I heard Ian faintly yell with his sweet Irish accent, "Don't give up, California! Climb back on! Don't let the bastard win! You're not off yet!" Ian was in the middle of his punishing hour of posting trot without stirrups. I could see him over Bushman's neck. He was waving. That was all I needed. Struggling for balance, I started to climb back to the saddle. Bushman never moved. Harry abruptly stopped laughing.

I pushed and clawed, and the hottest horse in the barn stood quietly, waiting. Finally with one last grapple and heave I was back in the saddle. I picked up my reins and cantered over to Harry. The man stood there dumbfounded. A look swept over him; a mix of compassion and admiration. Harry stroked Bushman's neck and then said sadly, softly, "You never give up, eh California? How did you get to be this way?" I didn't answer him.

After that day Harry was kinder to me—not great but better. I never did fall off during my training at The Vale. I was one of the few who never did.

When it was time to return home with my teaching certificate in hand, Harry approached me hesitantly, no marching clacking boots, to say good-bye. Strangely, there were tears in his eyes. He hugged me tightly, which surprised me greatly. His voice quivered like an autumn leaf about to be released for the final twirl to earth. "Good-bye Martino. You are a very lucky girl. You are a good rider. Think about me. Don't fall off and get hurt!" Then he let go and was gone, once again marching away in shiny ebony boots.

A few moments later Ian walked up. He had witnessed this unexpected farewell from Harry. "Wuueeee! What do you make of that, Ian?" I asked.

My dear friend answered. "California, you don't have nobility in America, but the English still do. Harry is to inherit a great title when his father dies. His family doesn't want him to ride. They want him to attend law school or something. They think his riding and teaching are stupid."

I watched Harry as he walked away. How sad that he could not do what he loved. He was a tremendous horse person, talented, soft, and bright with his horses. He handled horses with love. But Ian's explanation helped me understand the bitterness and anger that I had felt from Harry all this time. Harry had been jealous of a girl whose father had supported her dream.

I went home to California and the spicy smells of the summer country. Home to Pop and Mom waiting excitedly at the airport. Pop was proud of my achievement, my ability as a horse person. He held me tightly to him.

Two weeks later I got a letter in a light-blue airmail envelope from my friends in England. It was about Harry. Last Monday Harry had taken out his revolver and with his pet dog as his only witness had shot himself in the head. He had killed himself instantly in the high stone castle of his ancestors, in the bedroom of his mother and father. I wept for this sad man who never got to live his dream.

Twenty years later I lay in my house trailer, leaking blood from the impact with the post. Friends stood at my side in the bright autumn of the Pacific Northwest, their sweet faces looking confused as I mumbled, "I do think of you Harry."

Teresa and Stoat with grooms at the barn

The Warrior

I first met Stoat in a dank, gloomy barn. He was a thin dark-gray gelding with a white mane and tail, a striking combination. A cut on his hind leg was filled with raw and festering flesh, the result of a trailer accident. The gelding had never been turned out to play and he wore an expression of anger and injury.

In the beginning, I affectionately called him Gray Colt, but in time he would be named The Corinthian, his official competition name. Horses get at least two different names: their barn name, which is a term of endearment or a descriptive name; and their second name, a competition name. For this special horse, I also gave him a nickname, Stoat, after the smart, fierce white weasel that lives in the North.

I was nineteen and just back from England where I had completed my training for a teaching certificate. The horse's owner, Pat, had asked me to start her colt under saddle. When I began working with him, Gray Colt went through his training like he had read all the same horse books I had read as a child.

The first time I rode him, he softly turned around, curiously watched, and then moved off with a willing grace. Gray Colt was a good mover and trotted lightly on the ground. Pop observed, arms folded under his chin as he leaned on the fence. This horse was pleased that Pop and I thought so highly of him.

About two weeks later, in the midst of Gray Colt's training, Pop's heart gave out and he died. After that I walked through my days with horrible memories of Pop's death. Again and again I recalled my mother cradling his dead body in her arms, my hand touching his still-warm cheek where life had just been. Bruises had darkened Pop's mouth into a purpling kiss where the emergency room crew had tried to pull his wavering life back. The doctor apologized for Pop's death. The nurses, shocked and red-faced, watched us mourn in the emergency room as I had held Pop's hands that slowly cooled and stiffened. I couldn't forget his face as it turned glacial frozen.

In death, the spirit or energy that binds the cells together in an organized whole must flee like herds of deer running from a burning forest. Touching the flesh of a person or animal who is dead belies the wonder that is gone.

After Pop's death, I immediately went back to work with the horses. I rode Gray Colt and other horses, jumping furiously, not caring what happened. In the speed and the risk of the horses my pain and grief momentarily fled.

I challenged Death as my enemy and threw myself at her. Death didn't want me, but I wanted to approach Death so I could smack her with my hand and see her turn in my direction, snarling like a leopard. Still, Death ignored me as the wolf ignores the elk bull in his prime. Strangely, I was safe in the depths of my grief.

Every big fence I jumped was a coup counted on Death. I became like the ancestors, the warriors, who would run up to an enemy and touch him. That was the honorable way of making war.

Gray Colt, now Stoat, became my partner as I searched for the path out of grief. He was a comfort, a companion, and my wings that let me leave the world. Stoat and my dog, Stubb, became the pillars that supported my struggling spirit.

Mother sank down from life into something close to madness. She struggled with her pain and loneliness, abandoning everything else. Mother's anguish of abandonment made me doubt hope in love and life. I no longer trusted the circle of life—the rhythmic coming and going and changing of all things. Before Pop's death I had learned to watch and trust the circle of life. Not now.

My Grandmother Connie offered sage advice about death and loss. She had lost two sons in World War II and four young children to disease. She advised, "You must concentrate on the living." But that was difficult as my mind swam in sorrow.

It was the horses that brought me back to trust. Daily I watched and felt the bones of the horses dancing under their flesh. Bones that one day would lie exposed. Stoat lifted up my grief enough every day so that my heart could keep beating. And in that twisting kaleidoscope of pain and vision there was a feeling that rose up like a twig in the rush of water.

One day Stoat's owner, Pat, came out to watch me ride her horse. A tall thin woman with curling dark hair, Pat had a beautiful face. She also had separateness like a pale lily that grew bewildered among sharp rocks.

Pat stood at the rail watching silently as I rode Stoat. My body sensed something old and heavy approaching with loss in its hands. Finally, Pat said, "I've got to sell him, Teresa." Then she looked away. Watching her somberly, my only answer was the darkness in my eyes. My mind raced to the past when Stoat stood in a dirty stall, his water stagnant, his leg cut and unhealed. In that moment I knew that he was the only horse that I would steal if he were sold.

Stoat has to be mine, I told myself. My voice cracked as I asked, "How much?"

Pat turned back to look at me and said, "Seven thousand dollars. Do you think that is fair?"

I nodded before I could stop myself. Stoat was a magnificent colt. Then Pat walked away, picking up gear to take home to clean. For a long time I sat there on Stoat's back thinking, *Seven thousand dollars! There was no way such a sum would materialize.* Mom was broke and I lived hand-to-mouth. Yet, I knew Stoat was everything—the whole world's beauty and hope. My own life mattered little to me.

Later that evening Mom and I sat at the yellow kitchen table, the corners broken and peeling, trying to figure out a way to buy Stoat. Mom's face looked stretched and tired. She had $1,000 that she could give me. This was her way of honoring Pop's idea that our family could always have horses. I could scrape together one thousand more. That was all we had to carry my heart. As for Mother, there was nothing to carry hers!

The world puts life in your path, strange and bright. We complain and fret about the hard places on the trail as we climb up mountainsides, but we fail to see where the world puts a spring rushing down with foaming water to refresh us. Or at the high points, we'll miss an extraordinary view with green vistas rolling out into far forests of mystery. But we have to climb to get to them.

Yet, at that time in my life my forests were burning with the fire that makes pines explode. I could not find the cool springs to rejuvenate my spirit—and certainly, this search would be impossible without Stoat.

One sunny day when Stoat's owner was watching me work, I brazenly rode up to the rail. "I want to buy him," I said bluntly. "He is very important to me, but I only have two thousand. You could get a lot more for him." My throat seized up and I could say no more.

In my silence I looked down at the sparrows as they chirped and jumped, making a crisscross pattern in the dust. Then I looked at Pat. Her expression was serious. For a few moments she watched my callused, brown fingers nervously twirl Stoat's white mane until it curled like sea foam. Stoat and I were like earth and sea.

When I glanced down at my hands, rough from never wearing gloves, I thought of Pop saying, "One day you'll be grateful for calluses." I was grateful.

Pat stood still with her thoughts, then looked up at me, squinting in the bright canary sun. After one long, deep dry breath, she conceded. "All right, he's yours for two thousand."

Then she walked away. A few strides later she slowly turned back, stirring the powdery dust with her white tennis shoes. "You know, he was always yours. I knew that as soon as I saw you ride him." She whirled back and walked quickly to her car. I felt no sudden silly shock of happiness. No yell of joy flew from my throat. Stoat was mine, he always would be.

There are few horses who have held me, owned me in partnership. When horses are treated kindly with respect and love, they will show their sentience. Stoat's dark eyes were full of personality, curiosity, and wonder. Behind his soft eyes there was a spirit, a soul that could see into the distance like an eagle.

Stoat showed me this part of himself. He was part of my body, not just a limb. He was my eyes, my lungs pulling the sweet air deep. We were one spirit in two bodies. If I had painted a picture of Stoat, he would have been the glow around the sun, or the lightning stick of Coyote.

Stoat always called to me when he campaigned at a horse event. Whenever I walked out of his sight, he would yell out in a ringing neigh as he stood in his stall. He trusted me beyond the safety and companionship of other horses. If I had asked Stoat to jump off a cliff with the sea waving far below, unquestioningly he would have jumped. As he leapt, Stoat would have thought that I knew the strange water landing would hold good footing. Whether Stoat gave his bravery to me and I drank it in, or whether we shared this back and forth between us, I did not know. But on his back anything was negotiable, even the pain of death.

With Stoat there was no need to explain my grief. He read my sorrow from my body. And he knew that the healing was our companionship.

Stoat loved his work as a cross-country competitor and the success of my career was carried on his legs and black hooves. His bravery and skills as a horse brought me clients and gave me my merits as a professional trainer. The great teachers noticed us, including coaches and riders for the Olympic teams. I rode Stoat with the best in the horse business. Notable trainers admired Stoat's courage and my crazy, seat-of-the-pants riding.

From the beginning, my coach wondered if Stoat would stay sound, if his legs would hold up to the tremendous pounding of the work. He had slender legs and a burly body, which could cause problems. I watched closely and cared for Stoat's legs.

The first courses I jumped with Stoat were whirlwind runaways. He pulled at his bridle and did not listen to me. He ran at his fences with a fierceness that swept me along with him in ferocious wildness. I was caught up in his emotion.

The second cross-country course Stoat ran, my mother and brother came to watch. They stood with a crowd under a hoary old oak tree and waited for my approach to a nearby fence. We came galloping at thirty-five miles per hour, way too fast. Stoat's blood was up like the lion's when the antelope runs. He would not slow.

The fence was a pond of green water about five inches deep and a little log to pop out over. The rule with water jumps is to enter slowly, and when engaged, push to get out because the water creates a great deal of drag. We did exactly the opposite.

I wanted to turn Stoat away before we entered the penalty zone that surrounded the obstacle so we could organize. But Stoat had other ideas. His head was high and his nostrils blew wide, spraying snorts with every bound he took. I struggled, and finally managed to turn him. When I looked up, we were spinning through the crowd. I saw the faces of my mother and brother swimming in the congregation. My brother looked alarmed but Mom smiled confidently. Like Stoat, she believed in me. If her daughter was plowing through the audience, it must be the right way to do it!

Another woman didn't see it this way and screamed in a lazy slow way. Someone else shouted, "Heads up!" Circling, I managed to slow Stoat down without trampling anyone and then approached the fence with considerably less velocity. Stoat was extremely happy, never considering the danger jumping at high speed brings. He won that event and I was kidded about it for months.

During that first year of cross-county training, as the fences grew higher, Stoat learned his trade and began watching his jumps closely. I was amazed at his ability to read fences and figure out what to do with the puzzle of timber over undulating ground.

On Stoat I found out what the bond between a soldier and a warhorse could become. Through him I learned why warhorses of old were never for sale and why people would steal them or kill for them. These horses gave themselves to their people in such a way that it made human loyalty seem pinched and miserly.

Two of my old teachers had fought on horseback during the First World War. One of them called me, "the lion's cub" as I listened to his stories. Horses! I wanted to hear of charges and bravery that at first taught courage and stamina, but later delivered sadness and a hatred of human brutality and death. For the warhorses I have asked, *Forgive us for the part you played in our wars!*

Like all good upper-level horses who are loved and admired by their riders and crew, Stoat developed an attitude more like an imperious Caesar than a benevolent subject. Yet, with me, Stoat could be sweet and gentle. He lightened my heart and let me get away with silly things. I would put hats on his head and he would treat four playful humans to a bouncy walk on our way to a clinic.

Stoat showed me laughter in the midst of grief. We had a little game we played. I would pinch his soft gray nose gently and then pat it, much like a colt playing. Stoat's eyes would soften with playfulness and he would poke and peck at my hand—not nipping, but nudging and prodding. We would bat back and forth in a charming way to the amusement of the barn.

During our first five competitive years, Stoat and I won our first two runs, then moved up the levels quickly. We brought back silver and colored cloth to hang in my office. Over the next two years Stoat and I matured into our sport. Stoat's courses became art. Stoat's strides equaled the cutting strokes of the sculptor's chisel that slices into the stone, just so deep, but no further.

As we ran we became partners, our lives entwined. His ideas and opinions I trusted. If we were close to a fence and Stoat had a different idea than I did about how to jump it, I would let him decide. In time, I decided that Stoat owned the last five strides to the fence. Like all geniuses, Stoat was eccentric and possessed an electric intelligence.

In my grief I had looked for Death but she had ignored me. And then when I least expected it, she leapt out and almost had me. In the end, I lived, but I fractured my back.

I was gearing up to try out for the U.S. Olympic team. During a cross-country clinic, Stoat and I were jumping a coffin combination. It consisted of a fence on the rim of a gulch followed by a ditch somewhere in the deepest part of the gully and a final fence on the opposite rim. We jumped these fences carefully and then pushed every stride to get out. On this particular run Stoat and I jumped in too fast and ran out of distance turning over the second element. This was a big error.

I flew off Stoat's back, hit the wing of the fence and bounced to the ground. Stoat flipped over the fence and then, looking shocked, scrambled to his feet. Stoat turned back for me, and without much thought, I leapt up and looked him over. He was unhurt. Vaulting back on Stoat, I sat trembling. Something was wrong. There was a sharp dull ache in my side and back, and it was hard to breathe.

Drosk, the assistant trainer and a close friend, rushed over, her blonde hair flying. "Are you all right?"

I looked at her in a daze. "I don't know."

Susan, the clinician, scrutinized me. "Are you okay?" she asked, squinting and impatient. She was an old team member fit as a rod of iron wrapped in leather. The fall had been hard. I felt numb and queasy, but Stoat and I jumped the combination again, and finished the clinic.

As we drove the rig back home the pain intensified. My insides weren't right. Pain mixed with a sloshy sensation. At that point in my life, my aversion to the medical profession was at an all-time high, in part from seeing too much death in hospitals. I avoided medical help. Instead, for two days I walked hunched up and I couldn't eat. Secretly, I began to cough up blood.

Fearful for my life, friends drove me to a hospital. When I got there, I argued with the doctors. After a brief stay, I limped out of the emergency room with doctors and friends trailing behind me. My friends insisted on taking me to another hospital they thought would better suit me.

At the second hospital, a young intern distracted me from my pain and my aversion to doctors by asking for my opinion about his dogs. During the examination he found that my back was fractured and five ribs had snapped. There was a bizarre bubble in my back where one lung had been scraped by a rib, causing air to leak out of my lung like an old inner tube. After the exam, the doctor declared, "You are lucky to be alive." Grimly, I stared at him.

I tempted Death with my recklessness. Through Stoat's borrowed courage, I reached out to Death and touched her face. I found that Death was not an ugly withered monster but rather more like a leopard, beautiful and dangerous. My fleeting brush with Death showed me that Life was precious and it would never come back like this again.

With time, I healed from my injuries, both body and spirit. My pain told me I was alive. And this life, for all I knew, was the only one I had. Now I was determined not to waste it.

As for Stoat, this accident gave him a new found respect for his fences that he desperately needed. He never made that error again.

Best Run

The young woman sat on the restless chestnut thoroughbred and circled the start box, waiting to begin the second phase of the cross-country event. The sky, dark with clouds, was as threatening as an avalanche. Rain churned up the muddy earth. Nearby, the starter and the timers sat under their dark umbrellas, joking. Like clockwork, they would shout out warnings to riders waiting to begin their runs.

"Five minutes number twenty-seven!" With the announcement of our number, I pulled The Corinthian down from a canter after a warm-up jump over a big oxer in the deep mud.

I caught the glance of the nervous woman who looked like a frightened girl, her face crimped with emotion as she waited. She grinned and nervously asked, "How do you think the course is riding? Okay?" Her voice jumped like a hooked trout.

"Good," I answered in a bright voice, offering courage in the face of her fear. "I hear there's a hole by fence seven, but ride it to the left and push hard up the hill and you'll be fine."

"Thanks," she responded, trying to stay calm.

The relentless rain plastered down her light blond hair. Number twenty-nine looked pale against her blue jersey turning black with rain. Her white breeches on her slender frame were covered with mud kicked up by the horses.

Suddenly, the rain softened to a mist. "Is this your first time at Intermediate?" I asked her softly as we waited at the start box. She swallowed and nodded with a quick jerk of her head.

"Keep breathing deeply," I suggested, "all of us are nervous." The girl stroked her horse's neck and looked at me. "You're next," I said. "Good luck." Within minutes she was off, racing toward her destiny.

This was my first season at the Intermediate level with The Corinthian, the gray gelding Pop and I were working with at the time Pop died. The Corinthian was nearly ten years old now, and I was in my late twenties. We were old partners and knew each other well. Our years of riding together had taken us to only one step below the Advanced level, which is the Olympic level in eventing.

Stoat, my affectionate name for The Corinthian, ran cross-country like the twister that my Granny used to talk about—the one that took the chimney off her roof and moved the neighbor's house down the dirt road. Stoat's power swirled up the earth when he ran. He was kin to the horse in the Book of Job, who rejoiced in his strength and laughed at the armed soldiers.

The starter gave me a two-minute warning. I reached down into Stoat's body and spirit, and the world with all its worries, expectations, and triumphs vanished. The only thing left was the mist, mud, and the big gray horse. This was the meditation of the hunt, the silent thinking of the stalk, the run and the leap of the panther.

The course stretched for two miles over hills, through water, and beyond a variety of twenty-eight solid obstacles meant to frighten or invite. If we went too slowly we were penalized. If we went too fast, especially in the deep footing, we could fall. The winner would be clever, fast, brave, and lucky. The cross-country course was like life.

"One minute," said the starter somberly. I checked my equipment and tightened the girth. My groom, Karen, and the assistant trainers, Beth and Drosk, waited and watched silently by the start. They were serious and casual at the same time. Carefully, I bridged my reins, folded one neatly under the other, resettled my feet in my stirrup irons and circled the box.

"Thirty seconds." Stoat was light on his feet, but always the warrior. He did not waste his energy.

"Fifteen seconds." Stoat and I entered the box smoothly and turned around facing out. The course spread out before us, a landscape of open spaces and rain falling in curtains of sea gray.

The starter adjusted his glasses. The timers poised to strike the clock. "Ten…Nine…Eight…." Time slowed down, swirled around lightly, and fell like mist over the churned up mud of the start box. The leather saddle squeaked quietly. A white silence enveloped us and I could only hear the rain—and the countdown.

Under my hard hat brim, my eyes locked on the first fence, a big inviting oxer. Stoat felt my stare and fused his war horse radar with mine. "Five…Four…Three…Two…One…Go!"

I punched the stopwatch on my wrist as Stoat and I galloped smoothly out of the box to our course. The sweetness of that moment swept us up. The confusion of the world, all the paperwork of civilization, and the expectations of modern life stayed behind at the start box.

Stoat and I leapt into the moment full of hope and the raw turbulent power of a dynamic horse whose energy now flowed up under my legs and ignited my heart in a dazzle of electricity. This tingling flashed through to my black boots and back up through my hair in my black and gold helmet.

Stoat and I loved running and this fire ran back and forth between our bodies. Stoat's hoof beats sloshed in the mud and mingled with his breathing and my heart beat. There is a rhythm in a cross-country course. It moves like a river, surging forward on deep currents, then rushing and slamming through boulders. On this run, spray flew up in glittering arcs and the roar in my ears sounded like surf.

Stoat and I ran as one creature towards the first large timber oxer covered in flowers, bruised and wilting. Gallop, gallop, surge, leap—the shock of landing pounded up through my boots, and my head jerked backwards as we galloped on.

At the upper levels a rider must run on instinct because the course flows by so rapidly. If a rider has time to think, she is doing it wrong. This instinct comes from training for a long time. This knowing cannot be forced, and such talent cannot be bought. Sometimes I didn't know how Stoat and I communicated. It was like a single thread of conversation that ran between our bodies, as true as a javelin. This knowledge was boundless and quiet, small and powerful, and refused to be pinned down as merely psychic.

On this course we ran with instinct and my understanding of the terrain. I had walked it three times and memorized my notes. Stoat had never seen the course, but I told him what to expect. The position of my body, a half halt, was the call to attention. A word, "Easy!" and Stoat would slow up, knowing that the next fence was tricky and a combination. At times I would lean forward, legs closed, and growl, "Come on Stoatie!" He would prick up his ears and increase his stride, knowing that now the fence was a single big spread that required the leap of a lion.

As we ran, people stood behind yellow plastic tape on either side of our approach to the fence. Crowded under umbrellas, they watched. They were so close that I could have reached out and snatched an umbrella from a wet hand.

Teresa and The Corinthian

Stoat was good in mud and his horseshoes had big torpedo studs that kept him sure-footed on the slippery take-offs and landings. Stoat raised his head as we thundered down a hill towards an enormous oxer made of two huge tree trunks almost four feet high and easily six feet wide. Twenty strides out I slowed Stoat for a heartbeat, and communicated to him that the next fence was very big and that he must give it considerable room.

Softening the reins and closing my legs, the big gray horse flowed towards the fence. His ears pricked forward, and I caught his wild, sea-foam mane in my hands. Eyes in the crowd glittered white as they watched us flash by. A hush trailed our wake.

There had already been falls at this jump. Horses had come down the hill too fast and never gotten their balance. They hit the fence with their front legs and fell when landing. The mud was deeper now because horses had already run the course. But I was happy in my sweat and mud, confident that Stoat knew the danger.

As he galloped he raised his head, his hooves pounded, and his nostrils flared. Stoat began to switch his weight back to his hindquarters and bunch under himself, ready for the leap. We were seven strides away on level ground, roaring towards the fence like a tsunami.

Silence hung over the fence. Except for Stoat's rhythmic pounding hooves and our labored breathing, there was nothing else in our ears but the rain. I raised my eyes past the fence and watched the horizon to keep my balance up and out of Stoat's way. I saw the spot where Stoat would take off.

The strides rushed by. Four strides…three…two…then the huge push off the ground. I ducked down over Stoat's neck. We hung suspended in the air, free of gravity and no longer in need of the solid earth. We were hawks flying the thermal winds strong and confident.

Then, what seemed like a century later, we landed on one single forefoot. The shock pushed me back like a stroke and Stoat wobbled a moment in the deep mud. He recovered, and galloped on. The crowd yelled wildly.

Stoat leapt out of a combination in the trees and headed down the path to a tricky turn and around to another challenging oxer with a huge ditch in front of it. We flowed over the fences like water. The course was going very well. We were strong, fast, and confident despite the rain and mud. As we galloped, I looked at my watch bobbing on my wrist. We were near the half way mark and ahead of schedule by ten seconds.

The turn was coming up, a wreck of deep churned mud in the oak woods. We slowed down. The circuit had to be made in six strides, and then we had to increase our speed dramatically to leap the enormous spread of the oxer. Go too fast on the turn and balance can be lost. Go too slow to the oxer and risk the horse's refusal or a fall.

The landscape swirled around us as we advanced toward the oxer. We wheeled around one turn, the mud spraying up in sodden clumps. Mud grabbed at Stoat's feet and his momentum was shaken below the safety limit. My heart leapt up and I urged Stoat on.

We completed the turn but we were off stride by eight or so feet. This could be disastrous. Electric survival surged through us. Stoat recognized the urgency of the moment to "leap now or fall." There was no room for an additional stride. With a tremendous charge the gray took off early by six feet throwing me off balance as he twisted his way miraculously over the oxer.

My hands grabbed at his mane and one stirrup kicked free as we hurtled through the air. The ditch and tree trunks flashed under us. In a distant place in myself, quiet and still, I wondered, *Will Stoat catch a hind leg and spill over in a heap on the other side?* We hit the ground with a wallop and scrambled for balance. In a fragment of a second, Stoat heaved under me as he regained his balance with a shudder and then powerfully galloped on.

Stoat's shoulders surged under me and I felt his joy. He bucked a little enjoying his triumph at the last fence. His body rang out with exhilaration: *We are alive! There is something chasing us and it cannot catch us!* Then he settled back into his gallop stride.

Laughing, I glanced back at the last fence that almost swallowed us up. *You missed, Death,* I thought. And Death answered quietly, *This time.*

The fence judge stared, confused by my fierce backward glance. Adrenaline surged through me and lit my body like a torch. I had seen the deer escape the mountain lion and then leap and cavort in joy. Now I knew the happiness that these escapes brought. While I played with Death, I had tasted the preciousness of Life.

Stoat galloped on. We skipped through a one-stride combination and then headed down a steep gully with Stoat's head thrown back. He kicked up over some big logs at the top of the gully and rumbled down towards a large water combination. The water jump involved fences in a crooked line. We had to bounce over two fences, then down a big drop into the water. Two kicking strides and we were out over a thick log. We lined everything up in our sights.

Out of the corner of my eye I saw a figure running. I did not look his way as that would have thrown Stoat off his line. The man stopped. Then we were over the jerking bounce, and into a moment of peace as we leapt down the huge drop. The pound of impact, a fountain of spray, a drag through the water, and a heave over the last obstacle.

The man flew out in front of us and yelled, "T. Martino! Number twenty-seven, hold up! Hold up please!"

It was Peter, the technical delegate responsible for the rules and the running of the event. We pulled up, circling. Winded, I pressed my right hand against my ribs, calming an ache from an old injury.

"T, there's been an accident. We are putting you on hold. Your time has been stopped. The emergency crew is going to land a helicopter close by. Number twenty-nine has fallen at the big oxer and has been injured."

Peter's brown eyes were warm with compassion. Number twenty-nine was the young woman who had been so nervous at the start. I began walking Stoat so he would not chill. About that time my crew came running over the hill, looking frightened.

"Did you see it?" asked Beth. "Twenty-nine's horse flipped and fell on her. They are going to fly a helicopter over your head."

Concerned, I told Beth, "You may have to help with Stoat." She nodded. Two young girls ran up with a pen and asked for my autograph. This all felt odd, but I wrote "The Corinthian" on their paper and drew a little stick figure mountain lion behind the name.

My veterinarian, Mike, walked up. "Stoat okay?"

"Yes."

Mike smiled as he watched us pace calmly and evenly. "Stoat sure looks fit. He looks like a predator, a big cat."

In the distance, I could see the rider lying face up in deep mud. I recognized the colors of her jersey. Her horse was gone, presumably taken back to the shed rows. A flash of ice swept through my body. Was it her fear that crept up and spilled her? Did she hesitate when she needed to gallop forward? In my mind, I saw Death, like a lion, lay down in the leaf mulch to eat the prey. While I ran in joy with Stoat, someone else lay down in pain.

The dull chop chop chop of blades thudded in the air as the helicopter approached. Stoat threw up his head and gazed, a rare occurrence for a horse. Seldom do they look up into the sky. The chopper landed, spraying water up off the course. Stoat wheeled and half reared. I stroked him with one hand and he settled, glaring at the noisy machine.

The young rider was gently lifted aboard. It looked as if she was unconscious. I prayed for her and her horse that they were unhurt. The chopper lifted off, and the technical director yelled, "Five minutes number twenty-seven!"

With this pronouncement, I started to warm up again. Being put on hold during a run is a disadvantage. It would be difficult to gain back our fire and momentum.

"One minute!" Peter called out. We breezed through one warm-up gallop, and then the TD counted me down and we were off again. This part of the course was the hardest. The coach for the U.S. Olympic team waited by the slalom combination, looking for prospective horses and riders.

The next fence was a series of up steps almost four feet high ascending a hill. We set up our stride and bounced up the steps in fine form. Then with a great gallop we stretched through the large wet meadows, water spraying in our wake. The rain had stopped and we could see clearly.

Our next obstacle was a fence that was a large table with no ground line. We knew how to get to it, but it was so big and black it looked like a dinosaur sitting in the grass. Stoat flew over it in good style and we spun into the dark trees and pounded down the narrow track to a couple of simpler combinations. Then we galloped out into the open where a great hill spilled down before us in an ocean wave of grass.

The slalom was set on a hillside and had three verticals. Tree trunks with no ground lines were set two strides and three strides in relation to each other down the steep slope. The turns for each fence were brutally sharp and the angle of the hill made it easy to drift. The change of stride could result in a stop, a fall, or a runout. As we flashed through the grass, we started to slow up. At the top of the hill sat the coach for the U.S. Olympic team, observing the riders.

We galloped out of the trees and made the turn into the approach down the hill. Looking up to find our line, we saw once again a small figure running in our way, shouting. A horse was struggling to get up, and a rider was lying in front of the fence, dazed. She turned and looked directly into my eyes. It was Lisa, an upper-level rider whom I knew.

Things slowed down, but we did not stop. The little figure was a cartoon in front of me, waving, yelling, screaming at me to stop. It was the fence judge and she just as well could have been trying to stop the rain from falling. *Stop?* I thought. *Not possible. How could I stop the blood pounding in my veins?* Stoat and I would not stop again.

"Damn it, Lisa! Get up! Get out of the way! Are you hurt or what?"

Pulling Stoat down to a trot, I kept on our line to the first enormous vertical. Stoat's radar had honed in and as his ears pricked, he locked onto the fence. Lisa's horse was galloping resolutely away. Lisa floundered in the mud, all the while looking directly into my eyes as she tried to scramble and crawl out of my way.

The fence judge hysterically yelled, "Number twenty-seven, hold up! Hold up for god's sake!"

No! I thought to myself. *We were held up once already when Granny died! And again when Pop died! This time we go on into life.*

"Lisa, get out of my way!" I screamed. Lisa jumped to her feet and ran, unhurt, into the crowd.

We were three strides out. Stoat accelerated into a canter and with great strength sprang over the first element. We turned sharply, two bouncy strides, and flew over the second obstacle. One more fence! We were a hair off our line, the width of a lion's whisker, but Stoat nimbly saw this and again jumped early. The slalom was complete.

We thundered down the steep hill. A roar from the crowd followed us. My heart was a wild animal from that moment forward. The sunlight erupted from behind the dark clouds like a volcano. A fleeting thought slipped through me—quiet, shy, and as profound as a tolling bell. A voice whispered under my ribs, *This is the best run Stoat and I will ever have.* The merits of this course were not ribbons or silver, but the lessons Stoat taught me about life during our gallop.

Savor this moment, the voice said, *savor the thudding hooves, the brilliance of sunlight, the colorful crowds, the surging leap, silence, slam of the last fences. Relish the streak through the finish flags, and the smiles and yells of my crew. They are the tribe of our horse nation.*

In those seconds when I glanced behind me in the wind and the kicked-up mud, I could see far beyond to the riders and horses who would follow me, galloping into the future. Always, there is the circle. Others will follow our run.

Twenty-seven years later Stoat and I still gallop. We gallop in a hundred horses and riders, our students—those whom I taught, and those whom Stoat taught. When Stoat and I galloped we were free of fear and we laughed because, like the old European tales, Death rides a horse but it cannot catch The Corinthian.

The Secret of Life

The gray mare swung her body high in the air, and balanced on her back legs. She reared above me where I had fallen in the dusty arena. I had been riding the mare, Belle, in the covered arena at Cormac Farm. Suddenly, she reared to her full height and came down bucking, lost her balance and fell. I was still struggling to rise when she leapt up from the ground.

Belle stood a moment above me. In her eyes I saw something hopeless and dangerous. Down she came, striking with both front hooves, teeth bared. I had one moment to appreciate her shining coat and beautiful form, then survival took over. Rolling this way and that, I tried to get on my feet and yet stay out of the way.

The poof! poof! thump! of the mare's sharp hooves thudded in my ears. It seemed as if I moved in slow motion as I dodged her every move. My mind was strangely quiet. No thought, only instinct. Dust flew up in wide arcs in the afternoon sun. Something else directed my limbs, faster than heartbeats: *Go this way, now that. Try to leap up and grab her head or run for the fence.* But Belle was working with that same power and wished for my life. I couldn't get up.

A small, silver-gray form wheeled between us furiously barking and snapping. The mare leaped back, surprised. Beanie, my dog, had managed to jump the arena fence to defend me. She jumped at the mare's face and snapped in anger. Beanie's bravery startled Belle, and that gave me a few crucial seconds to get on my feet.

After one desperate kick at Beanie, Belle finally galloped to the far end of the arena. Beanie and I sprinted for safety outside the fence. Beanie, proud of her achievement, stood panting, her scalp neatly cut with a wound five inches long. Fortunately, the kick had only grazed Beanie's head. Although covered in dust, I had escaped injury. Belle stood at the far end of the ring and snorted loudly to warn me. Belle was at war.

Life brings me creatures who are down on their luck. A horse who was isolated and starved. Wolves who have been chained in a basement. Abandoned wolves and horses headed for the meat market. I have ridden hundreds of horses in all stages of work and of many different personalities. Belle was one of those creatures. By the time I met her, I had been a professional rider for about fifteen years.

One day in early spring, a slender, older woman named Elanor showed up at the barn. She was driving a truck and pulling a loaded horse trailer. Her soft English accent brought back memories of the gentle rolling hills of the country where I had trained.

Elanor shook my hand, and then took a deep breath. "I have a horse, a mare who is ruined," she explained. My eyebrows rose. She went on, "She was ruined by a man who beat her and isolated her and went so far as to starve her. I bought her out of pity, but...." She looked me in the eye. "I've been told that the mare is unrideable. She threw the last trainer several times and he broke his hip. I want you to know he felt that she should be destroyed, but I want to save this horse. I feel that people did this to her and that we should help her come back. I heard you do this sometimes."

The last sentence hovered between a question and a statement. Elanor's face was kind and serious. She held my gaze and I thought a moment before I spoke.

"Some horses can be saved, some are very difficult. You realize that she may be insane from the treatment she has received. If she fought the last trainer and won, she has learned. It may be too late."

The horse whinnied plaintively in the rig. The woman smiled sadly, "It was your barn or I take her to the vet and have her humanely destroyed. You're my last hope." At this she put her hand on my arm. The sincerity of this gesture was frightening. The decision was now mine. Either I took the mare and tried, or the mare died. A hundred thoughts flew by:

It's dangerous, walk away.

You have two, beautiful, new colts to start. Think of them.

If you end up a cripple, you won't ride anything again.

Two assistants walked up, Beth and Drosk. They had heard the conversation. As they stood staring, I could feel their belief in me. I couldn't resist walking to the trailer to peer in at the stamping, sweating mare.

"What's her name?" I asked.

"Belle," answered Elanor.

The mare was a dark gray, with a snowy white mane and tail. Belle looked at me with white-ringed eyes filled with fear and hatred. It was clear that this horse detested human beings. But then, I thought, *Perhaps she has not met real horse people before—people who work with patience and compassion, whose hands can be trusted.*

I accepted. The woman handed me a blank check to cover my expenses. Surprised, I stared at the check for a moment, but said nothing. We backed the rig up to an empty paddock. Belle was loose in the rig so we opened it up and she bolted into her new home. Then she stood and seriously stared.

Elanor looked at the mare sadly, turned, and gave me a soft, secret smile. She got into her truck and drove away. I took a closer look at the mare. She was a little more than fifteen hands high. Belle was mostly thoroughbred. She had a small short face, and big dark eyes under her snowy forelock. She was short in the back with big sloping quarters. When Belle turned, she looked like a bullfighter, quick and observant.

In the beginning, all we did was feed her. I spent extra time at her fence line watching. Belle didn't approach, but paced like a leopard. Then she would turn and stare in my direction.

In her eyes I saw danger for humankind. I know criminal horses are rare, and that 99 percent of the time they are created by the people who handle them. I know reschooling abused horses and wolves can only be done with love—firmness certainly, and no fear on the part of the trainer.

Could it be the same with human beings? There was a man who wrote me from prison. He described being in isolation and trying to keep the despair from his letters. But he was alone, utterly, and people on the outside feared him. I know this man had trouble when he went into prison, but now, after ten years in isolation, I wondered what this had done to his mind. *Can humans be born as criminals,* I wondered, *or are they like the horses and wolves, responding to years of abuse?*

After a month, Belle began to eat out of my hand. And after three more weeks of my standing patiently in her paddock, she let me touch her. The joy that day brought! She shuffled towards me, and I felt the brush of her soft muzzle. But after she ate the sweet grain, she wheeled away.

Two months later I began to feel confident that Belle's heart would mend. She let me brush her, and saddle and bridle her, though I had to watch her carefully. Belle could bite or kick. It was as if Belle was testing to see if I would beat her for bad behavior. But all I did was growl, and then she would behave, but watch me carefully.

Then came the day I finally got on her back. Belle stood still only a moment then bucked like a demon. She bucked so hard that my teeth rattled. She leaped up high and spun like a rodeo bull. I stayed on, fighting her urge to buck by trying to keep her head up and go forward. Belle was like the man in prison. She knew a lot about fighting.

An untouched horse, wild on the plains, is easy to train compared to a violent reschool who has experienced the wrath of humans. Over the years, these reschool horses have had to learn tricks in order to deal with abusive people. Belle knew many tricks; however, I managed to stay on until she was exhausted and stopped.

The next day I had my veterinarian look at Belle to make sure there was nothing physically wrong. Some horses buck because of back problems, or they hold their breath when girthed up. Sometimes horses can have a hole in their diaphragm that causes them discomfort. The vet confirmed Belle was in good physical condition.

Day after day Belle bucked. We would both finish exhausted and sweat-drenched. My neck started feeling like I had whiplash. Belle grew angrier when she bucked. I merely stayed on and this became infuriating to her. She was used to another type of war—the war between enemies, the war between slave and master. In our relationship I fought her with the instincts of a lead mare—a struggle, but not with cruelty.

I hoped Belle would respect me because she couldn't buck me off, and in turn would realize that I respected her because I didn't whip her for bucking. The young students at my barn called her "The Hell Bitch" since she reminded them of the bucking gray mare in the television show, "Lonesome Dove."

Generally, a horse learns to buck. A horse started correctly will not buck at the rider's weight. Getting on a horse for the first time is not the hard part of training; it is the years afterwards when the horse and rider learn to balance with skill enough to turn like a dancer.

In today's horse culture there are clinics that brag about starting a colt in a day, as if the quickness of it was the miracle. But old horse people know it takes years to create art. Horses as great masterpieces are not created in a day. An artist does not need to rush. I worked slowly with Belle.

In the old horse world, it was the apprentice's job to mount a horse for the first time, supervised by the master. This was because mounting for the first time was a simple thing to teach the horse. The master did the more difficult training that included the horse's ability to carry weight with the haunches and move under the rider with only a thought.

Belle had learned how to dump enough people to know a great deal about bucking. The challenge I contemplated was, *How was I to get her to stop? How could I teach her about the partnership between horse and rider?*

Around the same time that I was trying to figure out what was going on with Belle, there were other difficulties going on at the barn. One week everyone at the barn got the flu except for an assistant, Melissa, and myself. With forty-five horses to care for, we were only getting four hours of sleep at night.

I slept in a stall with a restless mare who was recovering from an injury. This particular injury required that the mare not lie down. Melissa and I took turns sleeping with the mare to be sure she kept standing. Between the flu and the hurt mare we were both exhausted. When we were at our wits' end, I had an unusual dream.

In my dream, Pop walked up the barn aisle as a young man with curly, wild, blue-black Italian hair. He leaned over the stall door and said, "Look, Sister, tie the mare to the ceiling rafters with the anti-cast roller before you lose your mind." Then he walked away.

The next morning I announced my plan for the injured mare to Melissa after telling her about my weird dream. She looked at me and planted her hands on her hips. Her small dark face twisted in mock anger as she sarcastically said, "Now your Pop comes and tells you! Why didn't he come earlier?" Then Melissa walked away, giving me one more teasing backward stare. I decided not to tell anyone else this dream.

About a week later, I called the barn late one night to see if someone was there who could help me. My horses, Stoat and Pepper, needed a bran mash since I wouldn't be able to ride them for a few days. No one answered the phone. Little did I know my horse concerns that night were mysteriously being taken care of.

The next day I saw the sponsor of the barn, Jane. She was from England and she was a woman of considerable means. Jane was also quite rational and logical and married to a man who was a top research scientist. Jane seemed strangely pale and quiet on this particular day. She looked at me oddly as I worked with the horses and puttered around the barn. For four days Jane hovered about as I worked and she got quieter and paler. She even looked like she was losing weight.

Finally, Jane invited herself to my house, claiming she had some paperwork to go over with me. We talked business for awhile, but something else was on her mind. She saw some photos of my family on my desk and one in particular caught her attention. In the photo, my father was a young man sitting on a horse in front of his old house in Woodmere on Long Island. He wasn't ready for the picture to be taken, so everything was askew.

When Jane saw this picture she gasped, covered her mouth with her hands, and almost backed out my front door. "What's wrong with you?" I asked, suddenly annoyed by her intrusion on my quiet afternoon. Jane shook her head.

"Something's wrong, what is it?" I asked again.

She sat down, hands over her face, and started sobbing. "God, I can't tell you." Jane was one of those people whom I couldn't imagine ever crying.

I put my hand on her shoulder, and again asked, "Tell me, what is it?"

Jane composed herself and got up. "You wouldn't believe me," she answered, shaking her head in disbelief.

"Sure I will," I said brightly, hiding my concern for her strange behavior.

"What is it?"

"T, look, I'm an educated woman. I am married to a scientist. Oh my god! If he ever found out, I would be so embarrassed." Jane grabbed my hand. "You must promise me that you'll never tell anyone."

"Huh?" I responded lamely, wondering what this was all about. She walked to the desk and laid a pale finger on Pop's picture. "T, who is this?"

I picked up the photo. "It's my father."

Jane sat down with a thump. "God, I had a feeling you were going to say that. Isn't your father dead?"

"Well, yes. He's been dead for many years."

She raised her face to look at me, teary eyed.

"T, I've seen him in the barn. I've talked to him. I think he's..." she paused, "haunting me."

There had been numerous problems in the barn, but this was a first. Jane wasn't exactly the type to see ghosts.

I paused, then asked, "What did Pop say?"

Jane answered slowly, "He said you would be late on Friday and to give Stoat and Pepper a bran mash because you wouldn't have time to ride. So I did and I didn't question him. Then he followed me to the stalls. He said that Stoat wouldn't stay sound and that Pepper was not brave enough to do the upper levels. Then he went into the feed room and shut the door. When I opened the door behind him he wasn't there. You know, there's no other way out of the feed room. I thought he must be a friend of yours—until I saw that photo. That's him! Oh god...I must be losing my mind!"

Jane slumped down in her chair. Then she added in a low voice, "If you tell my husband, he'll have me committed."

Jane looked at me, and waited for me to say something. I was curious. After all, Pop had been dead for nine years. "How did he look?"

Jane gave me a hostile stare. "T, do you think I'm telling you this so that you can have some strange family reunion?" Her voice edged toward shrill. "He's a dead man! I've been talking to a dead man!"

Jane stood up, and hurried to the front door. She turned, pointed a long finger at me, "You'd better just get him to stop!" Then she ran down the stairs towards the barn.

I didn't really want to see Pop, but maybe, in a way I did. We had been very close. For a long time I sat and puzzled over Jane. I wondered, *Had she really seen him?*

I told no one about this, but one week later I came into the barn office in the morning and Jane was slumped in her chair. She raised bloodshot eyes to me and said quietly, "You just missed him."

The barn was filled with the typical morning soft horse sounds, chewing hay, a stomp, a light whicker of greeting to someone bringing a treat, the slide of a stall door on its rollers, then silence. I wondered, *Was Pop's ghost walking like the specter of Christmas Past amid all the normal activity of the barn?*

"He was here?" I whispered.

"Yes," Jane answered solemnly, "he was." She looked terrible.

"What happened?" I stammered.

In a monotone without looking up, Jane said, "The office door knob turned slowly and the door opened. A moment later he walked in. He leaned on the desk and looked into my eyes and told me, 'I don't trust you! Because you are not Italian.'"

Jane slumped over the papers spread out before her, crinkling them. "T, I can't take much more of this." She raised her eyes to mine and yelled, "You have to do something!"

"What can I do?" I yelled back. "I can't control my dead father! Who do I look like, Hamlet?"

She leaned forward and grabbed my shirt sleeve in a desperate way, "Talk to him, tell him I'm not a bad person. The English love the Italians."

"Yeah, right," I said, sarcastically, remembering my training in England and the times when I did not feel that "love."

"You know something Jane? You need to see a shrink!" I left and slammed the door.

Jane's visions frustrated and confused me. Was she losing her mind? Did she truly see Pop? Could Pop come back? One thing was certain, Jane was upsetting the whole barn. If the sponsor went mad, the whole barn would fold. People were talking about her haunting stories and I was getting the teasing backlash.

The barn foreman, Carlos, met me in the barn aisle. With a bright sparkle in his eye, he matter-of-factly told me, "Terecita, your Papa is working on the tractor, he doesn't like the way it's idling."

At this, I rolled my eyes. "Give me a break, will you Carlos!" Carlos shrugged and walked away.

That evening I called my mother. It was a tricky thing talking to her about someone at the barn seeing her dead husband. I wondered if it was right to even have this conversation. Poor Mom, she had been through a lot losing Pop. At first, we talked about small things, then I told her Jane's story.

Mom's reaction surprised me. I thought she would scream or wail or cry or even laugh out loud. Instead, she calmly responded, "Teresa, if he could come back, I know that's where he would go, to your farm." She said nothing else and we hung up. I wondered at this conversation.

The next morning I saddled Stoat and rode up the hill, past the tractor with tools spread out around it. I wondered, *Had Carlos placed them there or did my dead father?*

When I needed a place to think, I often went to the top of the hill where the view spread out over the country landscape with its scrub oak, antelope brush, and yellow summer grass to the east and the Pacific Ocean to the west. Stoat and I watched the sun above the ocean. I spoke to the lazy wind, hoping maybe Pop could hear me. "Look Pop, I'm not sure if it's you but if it is I think I know why you're doing this. I'll be okay, Pop. I'm sure it's frustrating being dead, young, and not able to help me. We never did get our barn. But life is like that, you know it.

"I'm grown up now Pop, I can take care of myself. If you freak out the people at the barn, they might all leave and then

I'll have nowhere to ride. So it's okay for you to go on and do what you are supposed to be doing, whatever that may be. You're scaring them Pop."

The breeze stopped. Stoat stood silent with his ears pricked.

"If you really want to help me, tell me how to make the gray mare stop bucking. Then go on. I'll call you if I need you. And I'll see you later."

The little breeze came back with a lone falcon, surveying the landscape. My tears dripped on Stoat's mane. After awhile we rode back to the barn.

The next day I mounted Belle again and she started rearing. But this time, there was a new and frightening twist to her tactics. She would rear high and threaten, and then come down bucking. When Belle reared, it seemed as if she tried to lose her balance and fall. I began to despair and think that there was no way to reach her heart. Belle's owner, Elanor, did not visit the barn and she didn't call. She probably thought I was about to give up on Belle, who was one step from being destroyed.

A few nights later the coyotes who made their den by my house awoke me with their late night calls. Moonlight poured over my bed. I had dream.

In my dream, Pop and I were watching horses. The wild ones were jumping and leaping across the plains. They ran with the fierceness of fire and wind. Their aggression turned, by need, into the care of the herd. The lead mare, a gray with a long white tail, ran in front. Behind her were the other mares and foals, and in back, the stallion as black as pitch. The horses jumped everything in their way, creeks, ditches, and fallen trees.

Pop looked at me and said, "The way to reach Belle is by jumping her. Make her feel like a hero—the secret of life, Sister."

For a long time I lay in my bed and watched the yellow moon follow the horse clouds across the sky, jumping over the stars. I went back to sleep, thinking.

The next morning I built a low fence and lounged Belle over it. She devoured the challenge of the fence as if she were wild. Then she bucked and jumped with joy afterward.

After that, bit-by-bit, we jumped more and more. Something was shaking loose in Belle's heart. I could feel it crumbling under me when I rode her. Two weeks later I took Belle out to our cross-country course and she jumped like a professional over the solid obstacles. After we completed the course, I praised her and patted her sweaty neck. Belle arched proudly. That was the first day she didn't buck.

From then on, when I showed up at the barn in the morning, Belle looked for me, and when I left, she called to me. Belle's aggression turned to affection, softened by the partnership of jumping that mimics the wild. In time, even Elanor could ride her.

One year later some of Pop's predictions to Jane came true. Pepper made it clear that he did not like cross-country jumping, so he changed careers. Three years later Stoat tore a suspensory ligament and was retired with honors from the upper levels.

The last I heard of Belle was five years after she moved from my barn. Elanor was too old to ride her, so she gave Belle to a twelve-year-old girl. I saw them at a cross-country event, running like the horses in my dream.

It was at that same event that I thought I saw a tall, handsome man with curly blue-black hair at the concession stand. He turned and waved, and a moment later disappeared out towards the upper-level course.

Always

Always
always I feel them.
They move like a steady wind
that blows across the grasses.

I ride the old stallion.
His feet make a drumbeat prayer
on the earth.

He is like the old man elk.
His thinking is always on his wives
and his place.

He lets me ride him in the mountains.
He lets the wolves run with him.
The wolves follow us,
floating loosely above the trail
the way,
the way wolves go.

The sky I stare at,
the father, the grandfather,
the mother, the grandmother,
the powers, the earth.

I must stare. I can't see it enough.
It is so clear.
I must watch a long time.
I can hear the sea,
my old friend.

We follow the narrow trail down
to the open.
We all then feel the calling.
We turn and run,
this moment together,

There is no time,
there is no difference between us,
The stallion, the wolves, the woman.

Teresa and Gauguin

Gauguin's Truth

The horseshoe-shaped barn at Cormac Farm stood in a small golden valley surrounded by towering old oaks and deep groves of redwoods. High-timbered fences stretched up into the hills where some forty horses dotted the green landscape. At this competition barn there were two arenas, one covered, and the other an outdoor jumping ring. There was also a cross-country course and a hot walker.

For five years this farm had been my home and my life. I worked as the head coach and was paid a good salary and received numerous benefits that other horse pros often don't receive.

Many times I rode horseback on the high ridges with my three wolf rescues trotting beside me. From the ridges I would gaze at the expansive rolling Pacific Ocean for long periods of time, looking for something, sensing something as yet unnamed. I was twenty-nine years old and restless.

The great empathic dance between horse and human was part of my search. To me, it has always been an art form. Again and again, I find the truth of this when I witness a horse who comes willingly to a human without bribery or force. In turn, the human cares for the horse because the horse gave up his freedom. And a real horse person will choose what is best for the horse. With Gauguin, I experienced this pact between horse and human.

Jane was the owner and sponsor of Cormac Farm, and she supported all its endeavors financially. She was a practical woman in love with the horse business, and in particular, cross-country horses. My upper-level event horse, Stoat, was retiring and Jane wanted to replace him with another potential upper-level horse. This was good business for a professional barn. So I was sent overseas to Jane's homeland, England, as well as to France to find a prospect.

I found Gauguin in a top competition barn in Britain. He was perfectly proportioned, a bright clear bay with no white, and he stood a full seventeen hands high. He had tremendous scope over fences and a soft, wise, kind eye. Gauguin's price was $80,000. In a phone call, Jane listened carefully to my emphatic song of praise, then said, "I will wire the money."

In England, I closed the deal with a handshake, which in the old days was how people did business. Gauguin flew home in style, though someone stole his horse blanket and shipping boots in transit. When we got back to Cormac Farm everyone held their breath as the big horse proudly walked out of the rig. As I watched Gauguin, I thought, *How strange and innocent is the trust of horses who must rely on another species for hope of a good life.*

Three days later I met with Jane in her office. She sat at her big wooden desk, her blond hair neatly styled, and her clothes clean and pressed. How she stayed clean in a barn always surprised me. Jane asked for the paperwork, which I pulled out of my pocket in a wad along with wolf fur and lint. Carefully, she looked through the torn wrinkled paper. "Ah, T, where's the bill of sale?" she asked. "I need it for the accountant. I can't pay eighty thousand dollars for a horse without a bill of sale."

Smiling, I slowly answered, "You don't ask for a bill of sale. It's on everyone's honor. You shake hands."

Jane's jaw dropped open, her blue eyes widened. "You mean there is no bill of sale? We did this whole deal without a contract of any kind?" Her voice rose to a squeak as if she were a hunting bat.

"No," I responded, "it isn't done that way, really, Jane, I'm not joking with you."

Jane looked at me fiercely, "T, get me a bill of sale!"

So I called the former owner in England and explained what I thought were the peculiarities of my sponsor. He was sympathetic and said he would send the slip right away.

When we got it, the receipt read, "Sold to Cormac Farm. One brown gelding $80,000." Then scrawled at the bottom was a spider web of a signature. Jane was somewhat taken aback by this simple note but she said nothing. She merely read it and glared at me.

Repeatedly, over the years, I have asked myself, *What was it that made Gauguin worth eighty thousand dollars? His beauty, his scope? What is it that makes horses worth so much money? Was Gauguin more valuable than Stoat or the old, kind school horses the kids love?*

The horse business can twist love and beauty and art around until it screams. Is it important when a horse has a lovely soul? Or is it more important for a horse to jump big and bold?

At the barn the old school horses with their long teeth and sagging backs welcomed Gauguin. They offered shy whickers of friendship and Gauguin answered them back readily.

After a week to recuperate from his flight and the move, I began riding Gauguin. He had been started correctly, and I felt, gently. When Gauguin jumped it felt like a rolling wave. He was easy to sit and honest over courses. He was a joy to work with. Occasionally, Jane watched us ride. Gauguin was one of the few horses that drew Jane like sunlight and bird song from the dark of her office.

When the eventing season opened, we started competing, first in dressage and then in jumper shows. Gauguin drew stares wherever he went. People admired his beautiful movement and great jumping style. My peers would come up to our shed row at the events and compliment Cormac Farm's new horse.

Karen, the head groom, beamed at this praise as if Gauguin were her child. She and I brushed him until his clear bay coat shone with touches of gold. Karen loved Gauguin, perhaps more than anyone else because his sweet nature seemed to match Karen's own gentleness.

Preliminary level was a snap for Gauguin. He rolled over the courses effortlessly. Cautiously I moved him up to Intermediate level where the fences are bigger and more complicated. Gauguin ran his first Intermediate course in the green of Farhill in Oregon. This was a big course but built with perfect distances in between combinations. We rolled along over the Farhill course in fine style and the crowd cheered.

We had been first out of the box, and the course being new, people were concerned on how it would run. Ten riders started at Farhill and three finished, with no faults, including Gauguin and me.

The only thing on the Farhill course that I noticed as a warning was that Gauguin hesitated going into the water complex. It was a jump into the dark of forest and over a huge slanted wall. One stride and out. Then another two fences set in a bounce. Gauguin had hovered briefly at the edge and his hind legs rattled the back of the jump in.

I dismissed my concern, telling myself, *Gauguin and I are getting used to each other.* I had great hopes for our future together. My plan was to run Gauguin on as many different cross-country courses as I could out west before taking him east to compete at Radnor, which was the first baby step to international competition.

A month later, I took Gauguin to the next upper-level event, Wild Horse in Napa California. This was a much harder course. I had run this course many times with Stoat. The fences are big and complicated, and the distances are varied. This event requires a horse to gallop at high speeds, slow up to jump tight combinations, and then gallop immediately afterward. Otherwise, the horse and rider will not make the time.

At Wild Horse the beginning went well for Gauguin as we sailed out of the start, my crew watching. Then close to the halfway mark, Gauguin started hitting the tops of fences, knocking them with his hind legs. This threw me off balance as we hurtled over them. I thought perhaps he was tired so I slowed up, preferring to have time faults rather than have Gauguin exhausted and miserable at the end.

Coming up a hill, we galloped into the dark of an oak wood where there were two big wood piles. Not really a difficult jump but maximum height with an awkward distance between the jumps. We had to get in just right to take two bouncy strides in order to get out. As we approached, I slowed Gauguin to steady him, then pushed six strides away. We landed after the first obstacle and then eyes up; we took one stride, then two, and leapt out. But something caught our momentum. It was as if we had run into a wall. I was catapulted out of the saddle and airborne, almost landing on the fence judge.

The force knocked me out for a few seconds, then I struggled to my feet. I staggered towards Gauguin, who was standing in the landing zone of the second element. As I looked him over, I trembled. Gauguin had one huge scrape on a hind leg. I trotted him a step or two in hand.

The fence judge tried to hoist me into the saddle, but Gauguin was off, lame. So I pulled him from the course and slowly loosened his girth. We walked back to the start where I found my crew, pale faced and concerned. I had fractured my back two years before and they had heard our number announced and that we were down.

When Karen took Gauguin, I could see the pain in her eyes. Her love and concern for this horse impacted me as hard as the fall. I kept asking myself, *What had gone wrong? He was fit enough and strong enough. What had backed him off so he didn't commit to his fences?*

We went home, cared for our wounds, then started training again. Jane was calm. She realized that the horse was young, only eight years old, and this was his first season at Intermediate level. But my body began telling me with little quivers of nervousness that something was wrong.

Courage is mysterious the way it rears up against risk and danger. Courage can throw away tight caution the way a Masai throws a spear against the lion. In the best partnerships, the horse and rider give each other a confidence. To compete in upper-level eventing, the horse and rider must hunger for the jumps. In the upper levels, if a horse and rider are not brave, they can get hurt. The same is true if a horse or a rider is forced to compete beyond individual skills.

I have always prided myself in the ability to find out what a horse is good at, what he or she wants to do, and then allow that process to happen.

For Gauguin, who was a kind and gentle soul, we were asking him to jump the high and solid obstacles of cross-country. At the Intermediate level I began to feel uncomfortable with Gauguin. He did not have the fire and power of Stoat who ran like a tiger. I had known Stoat from the beginning, but with Gauguin, I had no idea what had happened to him in the early years of his training. I asked myself, *Had he been forced into water by a previous trainer? Did he get hurt the first time he had jumped into the dark? What did Gauguin think of people and himself?* I was uncertain of his level of confidence and whether or not Gauguin really wanted the life of cross-country competition. If he did not, what then?

One day I was schooling Gauguin at an open-water complex. He didn't commit fully to the leap and hit the top of the heavy timbered panel with his front legs and flipped completely over it. It was a slow fall, his great body tipping over like a sawed off redwood tree. I rolled out of his way as he hit the water with a great splash and spray.

Shock, guilt, and surprise shook Gauguin's body. He slowly got up at the same time that I staggered to my feet. In dismay, I looked at the fence. We had come in and he was hesitant. I had asked him to go forward to create enough power to leap the panel into the water. Reluctantly, Gauguin had obeyed, but not quite enough. He did not have it in him and so we had flipped.

Gauguin shook his mane and I looked him over. He was unhurt. Or was he? Dark-brown irises surrounded the dark-blue depths of his eyes, the little sunshade that nature gave the horse to see great distances in the bright sunlight. He stood calm now, but I knew he was confused, not angry. I took him to a simpler fence, a drop down a big bank with no water. He jumped this fine.

Event people all have friends, other coaches they can rely on to give advice. Brian was another event coach whom I trusted and respected. When I called him I asked to visit. I needed a peer to watch our problem. He agreed, so the next day Karen and I loaded up Gauguin for the six-hour drive to Brian's barn.

We drove the coast highway along the Pacific Ocean where the fog clung like damp moss to the land. Then we turned inland headed for the rolling coastal hills of San Juan Baptista where Brian had a competition barn.

Once there, I rode Gauguin out to Brian's cross-country course. The bright summer day was so hot and still that the dust hung in the air. Gauguin jumped, but there was a curious reluctance, a hesitancy. We stopped to rest a moment and I looked up at the sky. I thought of Stoat and his courage when we rode cross-country. I told myself, *Maybe you only get one Stoat.*

After an hour, I rode over to Brian for his opinion. As I sat tall on the bay's back, I squinted in the sunshine in order to see Brian's slim rider's frame. He took off his baseball cap and combed his light brown hair through his fingers.

"T, this is hard to say, but I don't think this guy has the courage it takes. It's missing in him. And you are not the type of rider who will slam a horse over cross-country by beating him over fences." Brian took a deep breath then looked into my eyes. "T, you want them to love you."

My eyes suddenly teared up. If there was one thing I wanted all my life it was to be an upper-level rider. I wanted this with Gauguin. The courage of a partnership and the challenge of the fences. For me, this level of art was the golden chalice, the sweet moment in the morning when I wake up and realize that today I will run.

Stuttering, I responded, "I guess I got it on Stoat and that's all I'll get."

Brian walked up close, his gray eyes sincere. "Every rider gets one special horse. Stoat was a brave horse, but ask yourself this question, Would you trade the way you feel about horses to be able to ride at the top?"

A heavy silence surrounded us. An ocean of thought surged through me, its waves rolling like a good cross-country course. Though I didn't know it in that moment, I was freed. My chains of ambition and glory traded for simple love.

After a moment of shock, I stated my truth: "I wouldn't trade, Brian." Brian was my friend and he knew the secret places of spirit. He opened my mystical gate to far freer pastures by asking my horse soul, "If you could do anything, what would you do, T.?"

Without a moment's hesitation, I answered, "Live in the mountains with my wolves, do art, and ride my pet horses, however they wanted to excel."

"There's your answer." Brian then turned, smiling, and walked away.

I patted Gauguin, he relaxed, and reached down to pick a dandelion with his soft lips. I sighed a breath of letting go. We drove back to Cormac Farm in silence.

The next day in the cool of the barn office, I sat with Jane explaining my situation. Her face was blank. Then I told her my decision. "What did you say?" she asked, shocked and stunned as any rider slammed into a stone wall.

"I'm leaving. I'm giving you six months' notice. I can't do this anymore."

Jane leaned back and smiled. "You're tired, T, that's all! Take a week off."

"Jane, listen carefully to me," I insisted. "Gauguin is not a cross-country horse. I will not beat him to make him jump big fences. He doesn't want to do this. Alexander isn't going to be an upper-level horse, either. He is a good sire, a jumper, perhaps a medium-level dressage horse."

Jane's eyebrows raised, and her voice tightened: "I spent good money for those horses and in good faith it's your job to make them fit into the program."

"They can't be made to fit, Jane. I can't either. If I try, I will end up crippling or ruining a horse I love."

"Okay. What will it take?" asked Jane. Now, her voice was like an immovable rock.

"Excuse me? I don't understand?" Now I was shocked and stunned.

"What do you want?" insisted Jane. "A new house? More money? What?"

I stared at her. Outside the office door horses banged on their stalls and called to each other as they waited to be fed.

"T, we are in this together," Jane cajoled. "You are this barn! I thought we'd be in this partnership a long time."

Her words rang sorrow. I heard and felt her sense of betrayal from me. We bruised one another with our words like boxers fighting. I didn't wish to hurt Jane, but she was as trapped as Gauguin, trapped by a system of conformity and money.

"Jane, you have six months to find another coach. Nothing you could give me will make me change my mind."

Jane stood up, her hands clenching the desk top. Concern now cloaked her tone. "T, what will you do? You have no other skills! You'll starve!"

Without another word, I walked into the bright morning that fell down free around me. With this revelation, a great castle in my mind collapsed. The end of a romantic dream where a child stood, watching great horses run. I had decided to turn away from the course. Now I was the woman who stood staring at the mountains, clear and bright.

In the following days, the barn grew cold around me. Jane hated my choices and their reflection on what she was doing. She hardly spoke to me. Her secretary, who had been my friend for years from the old track days, wouldn't even look at me.

My assistants, Beth and Drosk, and the grooms, Karen and Melissa, were all supportive. My clients, though confused, were as understanding as they could be under the circumstances. Some of them I had coached for a long time, and they trusted me when I taught them how to jump cross-country. It wasn't easy for these students to let go.

My horses were the same as always, unconcerned with my troubles. I took them on long trail rides with the wolves. We rode through the dry, golden autumn hills, high on the ridges. We watched the cold rough Pacific Ocean as the white roaring waves sped towards the shoreline.

Now that I was leaving the barn, there were tough choices to make. *What would happen to the animals whom I loved?* I worried. I had enough stock in the Cormac Farm corporation that I could save one or two horses, but not all. Five years earlier I had put all four of my horses into the corporation. That way I didn't have to pay board for them. It worked well. They ran under the barn's colors and made money for the farm. But I had not foreseen this outcome.

My stock would not allow me to take either Alex or Gauguin from the barn because they were worth more than I had. So, I suggested to Jane that Gauguin be sold as a hunter where he would excel. Alex could continue to do dressage and lower-level eventing where he would be comfortable. Alex could also continue to breed his beloved mares.

My dear school horse, Knight, had been with me for six years. Knight was an old dark bay who had to be watched closely. If he were ridden too hard he would go lame. *What would become of him?* I wondered.

My four-year-old black stallion, Ranger, Alex's son, would have to be sold. No one could work with him easily because he was temperamental. As for my beloved Stoat, he was worth quite a sum of money, even in retirement. He was an upper-level school master.

In our next business meeting, Jane coldly told me how much stock I had in the corporation, and what that meant in terms of cash. The sum came to exactly $12,000. Stoat was appraised at $10,000. To Jane's astonishment, I traded her my stock for Stoat, leaving me $2,000 to start a new life.

A great sadness surrounded this transaction. How could there be a price on this love? Why didn't Jane realize how important my horses were to my life? The horses were my blood and heart beating in my chest.

Before leaving, I visited Gauguin, Alex, Ranger, and Knight for the last time. It had been exactly six months since I had given my notice. When I stroked Gauguin's gentle face, I didn't cry. I had left horses before. I wished my horse friends luck. The barn would keep Alex and Knight. Ranger's future was uncertain.

When I said good-bye, I knew I was saying good-bye to a childhood dream. I had traded it for my truth and for Gauguin's truth.

Gauguin was not an event horse. He did not want to run at the upper levels of eventing. And I was more than just an event rider. Foremost, I was a human being who loved horses, and I was willing to accept them on their terms. I wanted that acceptance for myself as well.

Gauguin was quickly sold as a hunter for $40,000. Maybe he would be safe because he carried a high price tag. But a bitterness hung in my belly. How could a dollar value be placed on Gauguin? His owners would not let him just be a horse. My only consolation was that now he would be in a sport where he could excel.

For myself, I feared that I had traded my safety for freedom and truth in a world where these values are often punished. I was no longer following the norm in the horse business. There were no guarantees that I would be safe and not go hungry.

Now, the world stretched out before me with unknown courses to jump. But I was free. I packed the black truck with my few possessions. The wolf rescues crowded behind me in the club cab of Hot Black Desperado. One quick wave at my friends, Carlos, Karen, Melissa, Beth and Drosk, and I drove off without looking back.

The place I drove to was a little island in the dark waters of Puget Sound.

Ice and Paddy

Immortality of Ice

Sound Food, one of the few restaurants on Vashon, stands at the crossroads of the Pacific Northwest island where I live. In the spring, its gardens are heavy with wisteria, and crows and robins peck in the thick tall grass. Island regulars and tourists alike gather around old wooden tables with wooden chairs that scrape across the wooden floor, announcing their comings and goings. Everyone is nourished as much by the homey atmosphere as by the fresh, home-cooked food.

This haven is where my friends and I often eat. And on many mornings, early, I used to sit alone at a small side table next to a window and I wrote. The people who worked at the restaurant knew me and my living predicament. So, when I showed up for a meal, I felt like a favorite family member. They brought me food they had lovingly prepared, and I could stay as long as I liked.

In the first years of establishing my nonprofit for wolf and horse rescue, Wolftown, this cozy restaurant had become a second home—in large part out of necessity. I did not have a table and chair in my cramped living space in my small Airstream trailer. I did not have electricity because the trailer was old and the wolf rescues who lived with me enjoyed chewing on the trailer, bit by bit. The wolves liked to chew on just about anything, so I had to keep my laptop in the only safe place I had—inside the microwave, which didn't work.

One golden morning I sat at my writing table, alone, but not writing. The restaurant was empty, no tourists, just quiet. As I stirred my coffee, the spoon made soft musical clinks. The steam rose and the milk swirled through the coffee like storm clouds, lighter and darker. It was sweet, and reminded me of Pop and sadness and death.

The waitress, Ellen, came over and laid her hand on my shoulder. She gave me a hug. "I heard you had a tough day yesterday. Summer came in to get your coffee and she told us what happened."

I looked up, welcoming her comfort. "Yes, the black mare died yesterday. She had a little two-month-old foal."

Turning back to my coffee, and my hypnotic stirring, I sank into my thoughts, the ones I tell myself for comfort.

Remember the Mystery of life and death that surrounds us all....

Water is immortal. You cannot destroy it, for it will change form and slip away unharmed.

I sipped my coffee and I wondered at water. *Through whose veins had this liquid slipped as blood? How many bodies through time?* The coffee, made from water, had secretly crept through soil, raised from the ground through the trees. This water had been blood, urine, sap, sweat, nectar, tears, milk. It had risen through thunderheads, slipped down as rain, and been locked in the crystals of glaciers. Water had been Ice.

It must be hard to be a horse, especially in the business. The horse never knows if the people he or she is with will be kind to idiosyncrasies. A horse must wonder, *Will they love me? Will they beat me? Will I be fed?* Horses must trust that a human will feed them every day, because they cannot get out of their stalls or their paddocks.

Ice was a deep-black mare, over sixteen hands high, with a white stripe down her face and one white sock on her off hind foot. I first met Ice, whom everyone called Icy, at a horse clinic in Alaska. The owner of the farm, Julie, trained jumpers who were good enough to compete against East Coast horses. Icy was the daughter of Julie's first mare.

Ice was as hot as her name was cold. She was black ice, the ice that spins your car. I liked how Ice looked at me intensely, proud and tough. Julie had sent Icy to a farm with warm blooded horses to be bred, but the owners of the farm hated Icy.

She was difficult to work with, and hard on stalls. Icy wind sucked. Somewhere she had learned to grab the edge of a stall door in her front teeth and gasp air with a large belching sound. Her teeth put dents in the doors. It was annoying to the owners of the farm to constantly replace boards to keep them in perfect shape. But with a cribbing strap, which is a piece of leather that is worn behind the jaws in the throat latch area, this behavior can be prevented. At my farm, I didn't worry too much about cribbing horses because boards can be replaced. Besides, horses who are in pasture are usually relaxed with their friends and often stop cribbing.

Julie decided to send Ice to my farm in Washington to be bred to an Irish stallion. When Icy first arrived at the farm, she backed out of the van with such a roar and a clatter the van man had to jump neatly out of the way or risk getting stepped on. When I took Icy's lead rope, she twirled around me like a Spanish dancer, skirts flying. She neighed her announcement that she, the Ice Woman, was here. Then she jigged down the driveway to the barn, proudly swinging her ebony head back and forth.

I was taken with her strength, the black shine of her shoulder, and her dark intelligent eyes that looked like the dark cold water of Puget Sound. Watching the beautiful mare I wondered, *What thoughts were swimming underneath her gaze?* Her thoughts must be like great whales and salmon, strong and determined.

The farrier came out two days later and quickly learned to be careful around the big mare. She laid her ears back at him, pulled a hind hoof out of his grasp, and kicked him as a warning. Her blazing eyes communicated, *You mess with Ice, there will be trouble.*

After a time I began to understand Ice and did not force her to do what she resisted. I surprised her with carrots that were always in my pocket. When she was angry, I stood my ground and shook her rope, growling her name. But most important, I liked her and I admired her, and she knew it.

Icy began to settle and her personality flourished. She made the most amazing faces, and before long the kids who helped out at the barn began calling Icy "missile head." She would lay her ears back so far that they disappeared. Icy's head would become aerodynamic like a missile and with the same intent. She would push me out of the way with her head when I carried her grain into the pasture. Masterfully, she would get in front and block me with her shoulder. This became Icy's trademark maneuver.

After a month at the barn, it was time to breed Ice. We teased her into heat with Blue, who was a tall buckskin gelding whom I had saved from the meat market. A mare will only breed when she can conceive. Ice's response to Blue showed us that she was ready to be bred.

The veterinarian, Mark, made a farm call to oversee the artificial insemination. Semen from a stallion in Ireland had been shipped overnight, preserved in liquid nitrogen.

When Ice was artificially inseminated, she tried to kick the poor vet. I couldn't blame her. Artificial insemination work is strange, and I am not sure how to think of it. In a way, I fear the control it implies, as if humanity knows more about what horses should be like. I look at my beautiful, finely tuned thoroughbreds and then I look at *Inniskim,* a horse from the wild. There is a difference and the land always calls to the gene pool in a different way than the agendas of humanity.

Ice was impregnated and she settled down at the farm to wait eleven months. In the olden days a mare like this was the path to survival. The pregnant mare could still be ridden, and there was the promise of a new horse coming. A human could drink a mare's milk after she foaled, sharing it with the newborn. Watching Ice grow big awoke an old feeling in me—one that originates in my genetic inclination to care for horses.

Another horse at the farm, Sterling, became Icy's protector during this pregnancy. He was a tough little Connemara stallion who looked like the marble statues of classical Greek art. The stallion had a stand-up mane, and a small chiseled head. He was not a big horse but very cocky. Sterling acted as if the farm, its people, and its horses, especially Ice, were his. Ice responded in her aloof way to Sterling's calls with a calm whicker from her pasture.

As the seasons turned, Ice grew round. She looked stunning, a black mare silhouetted against the startling white snow. A motherly look came over Ice, reflecting the inner grace of the secret life growing inside her. *Inniskim,* the buffalo runner, would bow to Sterling's seniority, but he watched over Ice like a brother.

As time for the birth grew near, I told the working students about the risk that Icy would take. Horses normally give birth without complications, but when they get into trouble it is usually life threatening. In large part this is due to the length of the foal's legs.

Unfortunately, I had to leave for a scheduled book tour during the time when Ice was most likely to foal. And sure enough, a few days after I left, Icy foaled in the middle of the night while the students slept above her in the barn loft. The two stallions, Sterling and *Inniskim*, looked over their stall doors to witness the birth.

As the working students later explained to me, they were asleep in the barn. One minute there was just Ice, and the next there was a big chestnut foal. Summer and Caitlin went into the stall to handle the baby as I had told them. But Ice was angry and chased everyone off with the exception of Summer, whom the mare liked the most.

In the morning, with the birds singing and the kids going about their barn chores, Mark, the vet, came out to check both mare and foal. He later confided that the black mare had scared his assistant. Frankly, I admired the mare's anger. Icy was like a wild mare. This fierce mother instinct is what keeps a foal alive in a world where predators often steal new life to feed their own cubs. Many times I had seen this between the deer people and the wolves.

When I came into the stall to meet the new foal, Ice laced her ears back tight. But she allowed me to come near and lay my arms around the big colt. Admiringly, I spoke to the mare and she soon softened.

Ice and her colt were turned out into the large foal pasture. The working students, especially Summer, had sacrificed to try to witness this birth, and to help me while I was away. Summer was a senior in high school and finals had loomed over her at the same time Icy foaled. These students owned a piece of a common miracle and everyone loved the foal. They would joke, "What's Irish and lives on your lawn? Paddy-O-Furniture." So, Paddy became the colt's barn name. When he was an adult he would be called something glorious, but for now he had an endearing pet name.

Spiritually, I think of the eagle, the sacred bird who flies close to God, the Mystery. The eagle is holy but practices no ceremony. The eagle has no missionaries and no church, but the sky. There is no bible but the land. In freedom, the eagle lives without comparing and criticizing. The Mystery reminds me that everyone finds their own path to God.

One day I asked some students, "Do you want to do the horse rite?" Since we had a nursing mare and both students were girls, it seemed like a good idea. Nodding solemnly, they agreed. I learned about the horse ceremony from an old woman who raised horses, and then added some of my own ways. Although I am not a great one for group ceremony, I wanted to share this ritual.

I asked the kids to bring Icy and Paddy a gift. Something they had made. When they showed up that morning, they were bright and happy. I told Summer she was the oldest and longest in the barn so she would have to go first.

"What do I do?" she asked me. "Give your gift to Icy. Lay it in front of her on the boulder, then tell her what it means for you to be allowed to be a part of the horses. Then milk her into the palm of your hand and drink the milk. And after you drink the milk, give Paddy his gift because you are taking what belongs to him, his mother's milk."

I told them that to drink the milk of a black mare was important. To some Europeans she represents the earth. To some of the Natives, the black mare represents the inward road.

Summer's gifts included a decorated clam shell, which made me smile because it, too, was a symbol of the earth as mother. Perhaps Summer had reached deep into herself, and found an old symbol that connected her to the land. Summer and Caitlin's gift for Paddy was miniature, homemade patio furniture. Caitlin's gift for Icy was sugar cubes wrapped and tied carefully in a colorful cloth.

Summer walked towards Icy across a pasture of short bright grass with a sprinkling of chamomile flowers. Typically, Ice moved away when she saw someone coming. Ice would not let Summer come near. Finally, I approached Ice and held her head, soothing her. Summer presented Ice with her gifts. Then she tasted the mare's milk and exclaimed, "Sweet!" Then Catlin offered her gift to the mare and foal. With her head pressed against the mare's dark flank, Caitlin milked Ice, and drank a palmful. "It's sweet!" Ice gave away to the girls the oldest gift to humankind, milk and support for life.

We left the gifts on the boulder, already warm in the slanting morning light. I pulled out a few of my own hairs from my braid and left them as my gifts. As we walked back to the barn, I told the girls, "This is what women do. With women it is the sharing of the thing that draws mammals into a group. We feed our young with our bodies, and risk our lives giving birth. I'm not sure what men do, but I think they go with a horseman to a young stallion and get on him with no equipment."

Julie agreed to have Ice stay at my farm for the next year so I could get a foal from Ice, fathered by my beloved stallion, Sterling. He was ready to breed, and Ice had come into her first real heat since the birth. A stallion puts himself at risk when he goes to mount a mare. He is in the perfect position to be severely kicked. Normally, when horse people breed tame horses they hold the mare and the stallion to reduce the chance of injury. The breeders tease the horses with a tall solid wall between the horses, called "the teasing board." I imagined that *Inniskim* laughed at this because he had lived wild, and knew this way of breeding was far from the natural state of affairs.

Sterling was a virgin and actually, so was Icy. Her three previous pregnancies were from artificial insemination. So we proceeded cautiously. The young stallion teased Ice, asking her in his horse way if she was ready to be bred. He would stand in his paddock behind his teasing board and snort and blow loudly. He arched his neck, posturing. Sometimes, Sterling would rear and throw his body carefully up to show the mare how strong and wonderful he was.

At first, Icy pinned back her ears and swished her long tail, angry because it was not time for her to accept him. Her eyes would bulge at Sterling's screaming. But when she came into heat, she let us all know she would stand for the stallion. Icy would be carrying Sterling's first baby, and her fourth.

Those were sweet days. The rain had finally stopped and the pastures were bright. I was thankful for the grass and its immortal circling green. Every year I watched for that first hint of spring, then a flood of emerald. Grass fed the horses, and it was stored and baled for the winter for their bedding. And in the fall, I returned the favor by putting the composted horse manure and bedding back on the land so that the grass was fed and the land could hold water and not erode away.

One afternoon, about two months after Paddy had been born, Summer ran up to me as I was pulling out of the driveway. Her face was flush. "Come look at Icy!" Jumping out of the truck, I ran to the pasture. Icy's face was down low. When she swung it up to look at me, her head was horribly swollen. The nostrils were almost shut, and her eyes were hidden behind edema. Her body was covered in welts the size of half dollars.

"She is having an allergic reaction," I told Summer, my mind racing. I had Azium, an antihistamine, but I did not want to use it, fearful that I might damage Ice's fetus. Her breathing wasn't labored, and she showed little sign of discomfort. We led Icy down to her box, and little two-month old Paddy jigged behind. I called the vet and he confirmed my concerns that if I had given her Azium it could affect her fetus. Since the mare was not uncomfortable, we decided to wait.

By the look of two or three large lumps on Icy's nose, we determined that bees had stung her. A bee had probably stung Ice as it gathered the sweet heavy nectar of the new clover. We put cold packs on the bee stings and we gave her a bran mash, which she ate. There was nothing more to do so I went home to check my wolves.

An hour later Summer called and said Icy was fine but the edema was growing. I told Summer she could go home and I drove the five minutes back to the barn.

When I got there Icy was down in the position that makes a horse person's heart sink. She was rolling in pain obviously from colic, a severe stomach pain. *From a bee sting?* I wondered. I called the vet again, and then began gently walking her. When we stopped to rest, she'd stretch and moan in pain. Paddy wandered around, following his mother.

Ice began dropping little bits of manure, but getting no relief. My mind began sinking back to other sick horses. The little bits of manure were a sure sign of torsion, a twisted bowel. Icy must have rolled violently, which caused her to rotate her intestine into a torsion.

Horses have a delicate digestive system and sometimes a bit of bowel can twist or get stuck on connective tissue. As we walked, I worried, waiting for the vet. If Ice died, this would devastate her owner, Julie, whose own life was in jeopardy. Three months earlier, Julie had broken her neck while jumping a green horse. Now she was paralyzed from the neck down. Ice was the daughter of Julie's first mare, the horse who started her farm in Alaska. Julie had built her livelihood on the mare.

I looked at Paddy as he followed his mother around the paddock. With an inward stare, Ice shuddered periodically in pain. Possibly, it was too late for surgery. In that moment I regretted living on an island, too far from surgical help.

Mark arrived and we gave Ice an injection for the pain. As he examined her, he determined it was not a full twist but a loop of gas that the mare could not pass. We could not get Ice into the rig to go off island for additional veterinary help because she would not leave her foal. In her painful state, it would have been dangerous to take Paddy in the rig with Ice. With this particular type of colic, sometimes the horse will flip the bowel back over. Often, surgery is not successful with this condition.

The vet and I agreed that we had to wait this one out, as feeble as it felt. I called Julie in Alaska. The phone rang with a hollow sound. No one was home.

Armed with a massive pain killer, Summer and I stayed the night in the barn. We lay on an old mattress that the girls had used when they waited for Ice to foal. Covered with horse blankets, Stoat's old cooler, and my brightly striped quarter sheet, I lay in the darkness and prayed earnestly for Ice to live. An inner calm came over me. I knew Ice would die. I began to grieve for Ice and Paddy, and for Julie who was paralyzed in Alaska without her favorite mare. And for Summer, who had never witnessed death.

Life is brief and sweet and terrible, full of tragedies that are unjust and joys that are distributed like sunlight on everyone.

Morning came and Ice was standing. The edema in Icy's face was almost gone, but her eyes were dulled with more than the drugs, and her body was covered in sweat under her blanket. I covered her with a fresh blanket, held her head in my hands, and cried softly, "Don't die, Ice." But I knew if she did not die, the vet and I would have to kill her to end her agony. I called Mark again.

As we stood in the delicate morning, Summer, wrapped in the brightly striped quarter sheet, her legs and feet bare, I told her, "This is the hardest part about illness and dying. Someone has to be strong for the person who is going, at least while they can help. Then later, when all is done, then you cry."

Summer's eyes were dark from sleeplessness and grief. She said nothing. Paddy was locked in the paddock because I didn't want him to be hurt if Ice grew violent in her pain. Summer went to Sound Food to get us the false sharpness of strong coffee. While she was gone, I began the good-byes.

Slowly, I opened the stall door so Paddy and Ice could say good-bye. Icy nickered low to her foal. Paddy answered with a high call, and they touched noses for a moment. "Don't worry about him Ice," I reassured her. "I'll take care of him."

Softly closing the door, I went to get Sterling. He walked out of his box and neighed loudly at Ice. She gave him a soft answer and then ebbed down like the lowest tide into the dark place inside her where the pain resided. Sterling was worried and did not want to leave. I had to pull him along to his far pasture.

The vet finally arrived and after examining Ice, we decided surgery was impossible. We agreed that we had to put her out of her misery. The world is full of euphemisms about death. Full of ideas of life at all costs, but I don't agree with that. I have been in great pain, and relief from suffering is a blessing.

Carefully, I led Ice out of the stall. Paddy ran inside his paddock frantically. Summer quieted the foal. This moment seemed impossible. I asked myself, *How could I do this?*

In the midst of all of this, the vet's seven-year-old daughter had come with her dad, full of innocent direct questions. "Is she dying?" she asked.

"Yes, honey, she is," answered her father. Mark was a parent who was not afraid to let his child see death up close.

We all will follow Ice down the dark road that leads where no one knows for sure. That's why the old people called it the Mystery. Adults hide it from children because they themselves fear it so much. This little girl got to witness death openly, with her father close at hand.

Mark injected Ice and for a moment her eyes looked shocked. I stroked Ice and then stood back as she softly went down. I followed Ice to the ground. Tearfully, I turned to Mark. "I hate this part of the horses."

He answered softly, "I hate this too. Sorry T."

Somewhere my spirit raged at the Mystery. *Why is it like this?*

And the Mystery answered me, *You are finding out for both of us, for the Mystery wonders too.*

Ice the black mare, the mother of Paddy, was gone. The vet packed up his gear and drove off. Summer and I sat down together, next to Ice's stall. "Now it's finished." We cried. Summer held tightly to my waist and sobbed loudly and I leaned over her, my tears hot and silent. And as I cried for Ice, I remembered all of those times when someone I loved died. My mother and I crying over Granny, over Dad. The phone call when I was told B.B., my first pony, was dead.

Many nights I stand in the cold in the wilderness with my hunting wolves and yell at the stars. "What is it! Why is it like this?!" The stars turn and flash and become something else. This brings me peace.

For me, the hard thing was to let go of guilt. Couldn't I have saved Icy? Sadness is hard to release, but Death teaches me, *Don't forget to live.*

I remind myself, *The cup has been empty, it will be full again.* The unknown causes such fear, but I always want to be able to risk. It is through the risking that I learn wisdom. Through deep grief I know I have loved well.

"Look," I said to Summer through my tears, "Icy gave us a gift, though right now it is entangled with pain and we may not see it. She is teaching us life is precious and fragile. Ice was alive suckling her foal in the pasture just a few hours ago, and now she's dead." Summer had witnessed birth, breeding, ceremony, and death. Ice had taken her full circle.

As we sat there, Brenda, a down-to-earth woman, came stumping down the path to the barn. She had a concerned look on her face. Brenda heard the crying foal, and saw Ice laying on the ground, milk dribbling from her udder. Summer huddled against me. Brenda's soft words in that moment brought me great comfort that still soothes me. "I'm so sorry, what happened?" By telling the tale I found relief.

Brenda called the backhoe man, and then with sensitivity, she left us to grieve. The man came with a huge yellow backhoe and a troubled look as he approached us. Then he began to dig a deep hole amidst the green grass and white chamomile flowers.

"This is the next part we must walk through," I explained to Summer. "The good and bad of Icy's life with what we have left of her." Then we got up, willing to do what needed to be done. Summer made Icy a big mash because Icy loved her food. I got two flakes of hay. We gathered the things that Ice had worn in life—her bright red sheet with "Champion" written on the side, and her halter.

I took the cribbing strap that Ice hated to wear and in front of her sightless eyes with their thin film of dust, cut it to pieces with my tin snips. Then I held Ice's warm head and removed her stable halter. She would go to ground as she came. As I cut a strand of Ice's mane for Julie, I whispered to her, "Next time, come back wild."

The tractor driver gently scooped up her body to carry it to the grave. For a moment, I worried because I didn't want Icy to get scraped up and I didn't want Summer to see. I told myself, *It is better to know the truth.* As the tractor lifted Ice's body, I held her head and we moved toward the edge of her grave.

Ice would be buried twelve feet under where the earth is slightly damp. A flash of fear cautioned me not to fall into that deep hole with her. I stepped back as Icy rolled into the dark earth. After a heart beat, she landed with a deep thump that shook the ground.

Summer and Paddy stood slightly back from the edge of the hole. We dropped Icy's things into her grave where she lay in the gray gravelly silt surrounded by white chamomile flowers.

The first scoop of dirt covered Icy's open eyes. Summer and I winced at that, troubled by the act. But before long, Icy was buried completely. Standing above the torn earth a foal called to a missing mother, nosing a ripped, sweat-drenched blanket. The ancestors told me, "Don't disturb the dead we loved, leave them with peace in the clay with their things."

The horse children were warriors and the next day the girls who worked at the barn took the news with seriousness. Ice's death initiated them into a mystery deeper than their approaching puberty. Children recognize and respect the wildness of death. And many of them don't discuss this with parents or siblings, perhaps because they do not know parents may know this pain.

Adults admire young people and the strength in their bodies. We love their carefree days and deep sleep, but I wonder if it's really their wildness we admire and covet more than their youth. Young people can move in any direction like water.

In turn, the young must admire the old who have lived and fought, and who can point the way, building on the wisdom of life and death our ancestors gathered.

One day I saw a falcon who, while stooping down for a bird, miscalculated her aim and struck the ground. She almost missed the impact, but at ninety miles per hour the earth was unforgiving and the falcon broke her neck. When I picked up her warm body and looked into her black dimming eyes, I felt her life slip away, but I also felt her joy. Missed and killed while hunting.

My prayer to the universe: "Don't let me live a life called 'missed while sleeping,' or 'missed by growing so old that my falcon's body cannot fly at all.'" I don't fear the dark, I fear the cage.

Two months later I walked past Icy's grave to the high pasture carrying Paddy's grain. He followed me, cavorting, then ran in front with his cocky little head held high. Playfully he pushed me, and blocked me with his shoulder. His ears swept back, giving me his missile head look. I laughed and laughed. Tears slipped down my cheeks, moving from heart to moisture to water to Ice.

Queen of Heaven

A girl with an exotic face, golden skin, and long brown hair, stood in the doorway of my cabin. Her face could be personified by an antelope or a young wolf. Dirty jeans, a spotted T-shirt, and muddy paddock boots spoke of life with horses. Sarah knocked too loudly and with my consent stepped through the ancient cedar doorway, stirring up dust and slinking wolves who suddenly slipped outside.

I had become the older teacher, the one who left normal channels of civilization to talk directly to passion. In my simple life, I enjoyed the freedom of thought. Now, my life felt like drinking cool water in the heat of a stifling summer.

My specialty is eventing, teaching people and horses to jump cross-country over solid obstacles at speed. Young people find me, drawn to danger and galloping hooves. They test their strength and bravery by jumping the wise horses. When I work with children and horses I learn about the kindness of life, awed by the generosity horses give with their strength and bravery. The children teach me hope.

Mostly, it is my job to listen. That morning in my cabin, Sarah was sixteen in confusion and joy. "T, you are the only person I know who does what she loves. What should I do?" Sarah tossed her long hair, the bangs falling in her eyes like the forelock of a colt. Inwardly, I chuckled and looked around my simple cabin where I had to carry my water daily. Sarah did not ask, so I did not say that freedom has a price.

As she told me about her life nowadays, I wondered, *What will the world bring in fifty years?* I listened. "What do you think I should do?" Sarah insisted, exasperated with my silence.

Thoughtfully, I offered, "Plant trees."

Sarah rolled her eyes, "Be serious." Silence answered her, but she did not hear it.

A wolf came in through the doorway, stared at Sarah and retreated. My wolf rescues lived with me and were nervous around strangers. Sarah stood with her arms wide, telling me of some great dream. As she talked I thought of the wolves. *Will there still be wolves in a hundred years? What world do our children inherit?* I stood over the black wood stove and stirred as she spoke, watching her vision fill the cabin like the steam from the pot of soup. Passionately, words escaped free from Sarah's mouth.

"I want to ask you for help," Sarah stated after awhile.

I wondered to myself, *What teacher can resist?"*

"What do you want to do?" I asked.

Sarah's face was bright. "Not plant trees, but something wonderful. I want to jump my horse, Casey, over my mother's car."

"Does your mother know?" I asked.

Sarah smiled, "Of course." To hear this girl talk you would think she was an Olympic hopeful, and there was gold shining out there on the other side of her mother's convertible.

Sounding the part of the responsible teacher, I responded, "Thank you for coming to me before running out to do it. You realize you will have to train, and teach your mare." She nodded. "It will not be easy." Her falcon eyes locked with mine.

Inwardly, I felt the sense of the challenge, the hunt. Another wolf peeked inside the cabin to look at the strange girl. Perhaps the wolf sensed what had just transpired.

"When do you want to start?" I asked.

"Now," she said. Her eyes added, *I'm sixteen, there is no time to waste.*

My life seems unbelievable sometimes with the difficult choices I have made. Now I stood in dirty jeans in a dusty old cabin with wolves. No clean breeches and boots shined with effort and spit; no arena, no assistants, no comfortable salary. It had been two years since I had left my job as the director of a two-million dollar horse facility. I had traded my security for freedom and wolves on a rustic island in the Northwest.

The island allows for freedom of thought, but the island is a tricky place. From here, it's hard for the kids to compete in the horse world, or in the larger matters of the world. Yet, Sarah is the daughter of a mother who is strong and supports courage and challenge in her children. Hita tells them to explore, to take risks, and to make mistakes. And Hita takes her own risks as an artist, and I admire her.

All young things have a need to prove strength. The young wolf stalks big prey at first. The young stallion roams away from home and looks for coyotes to chase. This is the way to learn as quickly as possible what can and cannot be attempted. This testing helps prove the true trail of survival.

Sarah, and her friend, Jessie, had come to me once and asked about a rite of passage. In many cultures a young person needs to actually do something to be admitted into adulthood. I told them what I knew of such things in the Native tradition, which involved isolation and fasting in the wilderness. At first they were excited, then slowly, Sarah backed away from this idea, almost as if her blood called for a proving of her own making. Her European cultural traditions are forgotten, so she must make her own.

There was her mother's convertible. How wonderful! —to jump her mother's car. How fitting! As the young must always rise up and take the place of the old.

Sarah probably was unconscious of all this, but her spirit forced her to find something to challenge. We have separated ourselves from the natural world; we no longer use our cunning and strength to escape predators. But I have seen the deer leap and play in joy after escaping the lion. And I have seen the deer meekly give-away, which is the graceful sacrifice that life gives for life. In today's world we are not allowed to give ourselves back to the earth. Even in death, if we choose to be buried, laws require that we lie in a cement cocoon, forever isolated from the earth. No butterfly will emerge.

What course will we choose? If we fear death and do not see the circle of life, we will not risk like the young buck. If we do not respect death, we will fall into the grasp of sharp lion claws at an innocent moment when our heads are down, drinking. But this is salvation to the lion. To find strength, Sarah had chosen this leap like the lion chooses her moment for the hunt.

Sun on sand, dust flew up in distinct particles, as the blood bay cantered around the arena, tossing her Amazonian head. Perched on her back in half seat, the position used for jumping, was Sarah. She bobbed up and down in a graceful swing, half seat making her stand in her short stirrups above the mare's shoulders. Sarah and her horse Casey cantered the rhythm of a waltz.

The warmth calmed Casey, who was a reschool horse who Sarah had fallen in love with. Reschool horses are usually fearful or angry about their work, due to poor handling by previous owners or trainers. They require careful compassionate explaining about the life they live with humanity. Casey had a bright mahogany coat, and black points—her legs, mane, and tail all were black. She was tall with the proud, light walk of a predator, something that was looked for in a horse used for battle.

But the mare had not been taught to balance herself correctly and in the beginning leaned for support on Sarah's hands. "We must reteach Casey to carry herself," I explained to Sarah. "First, we'll make it easy, no rider." So Sarah worked the mare on the lounge line, a long rope, teaching Casey to balance herself without tension on the big circle—walk, trot, and canter. "A horse is like a person learning ballet," I continued. "It takes practice to move in balance."

Sarah had to teach the mare to slow her steps and relax. Together, Sarah and Casey had to learn the intense communication of voice, sight, touch, and thought that runs between horse and rider. The goal is to make each movement in balance count.

Standing in the deep sand, the sun rested on my back like a living thing. The teacher in me instructed, "Sarah, remember where the art comes from. The horse must balance herself and her rider in relaxation and mobility. The rider uses her body to talk with the horse. In the olden days our hands would've been busy with a sword or javelin. You cannot pull the horse around with the reins."

Sarah laughed as she pointed with her imagined sword. She lounged the mare over small jumps. Casey was excited and occasionally leapt around. Perhaps she, too, missed the dangerous thrill of the lion. After awhile the mare tired and we stopped, taking time to cool her out carefully.

For the next three months, Sarah continued to work with Casey, riderless. Sarah still didn't know that her test, her rite of passage, had teeth and claws. What could I do to inspire her? She told me she wanted to photograph this jump for her high school year book. Next year she would be a senior.

After training one day, Sarah and Casey returned home with instructions on walking for an hour the next day. And the following day to do flat work, no jumping. The day after that, walk. On the fourth day they needed to come back to the barn. Sarah sighed at my instructions. "What's wrong?" I asked.

"Boring, all that walking."

"You won't be bored," I said.

"Why?" Sarah asked.

Giving my diabolical coach grin, I told her, "I want you to do all the walking in half seat."

Sarah's eyes widened. "Sir, yes sir!" She responded firmly, then ambled off riding Casey without looking back, leaving me in the dust, in my boots, but on foot.

Back at my cabin, I was drawn to my big wooden trunk that holds the tools and the symbols of my trade. Years before, my jockey friend Dean had painted it white saying it looked scruffy. This trunk had followed me along many trails in my horse life. Originally from the multi-million dollar competition barn, it stood in a beautiful heated tack room next to a wall of ribbons and silver. After I left my secure life at the competition barn, the trunk sat in my pasture, and eventually moved inside my cabin. Now, I needed some symbols for Sarah.

Opening the trunk, I immediately found my black and gold cooler, a fancy wool blanket used to cover a hot horse. Black is the color of looking within, gold is the eastern light—a good symbol for Sarah. I continued to dig through memories, holding things up to the smoky light in the dark cabin.

Horse hair stuck to saddle pads, reins, and girths. When I touched the hair, horses from my past came to life. Equine eyes flashed at me and heavy hoof beats sounded in deep mud, where my exhausted breath mingled with old partners. My cross-country battles rang in my mind. Here is The Corinthian's smoke-gray hair—the one who brought me recognition in the horse world. And there was Alexander's hair, the deep-dark bay who ran with wolves in the hills and helped me find my freedom.

A jumping bat poked at my memories. It was the one I carried without falling in England to the dismay of the instructor who hated my courage. At the time I was an eighteen-year-old girl on a horse chasing an Olympic flag. At the bottom of the trunk lay my vest, streaked like the cooler in black and gold. This is what event riders use to protect themselves. It wasn't much. A symbol of modern knighthood. Yes, I was a knight, a warrior—a slender girl with long dark hair who, by luck, had been handed horses who were tough and brave. I was allowed to learn the lion's jump.

A cold black nose touched my leg, and startled me from my reverie. It was Mckenzie the gray wolf. I had traded my fences for her. Now I run with wolves. Instead of Olympic banners, I have hawk feathers and mountains. Mckenzie panted, smiling up at me, calling me back to the moment. I shut the trunk.

Sarah and Casey continued to train with me through the hot summer months. Sweat ran in our eyes, and the mare's bright coat darkened with perspiration. Sarah was tough, she did not resist my thoughts, my criticisms. She was like an Osage bow that I molded to shoot arrows at modern life, but she didn't know this.

When I first met Sarah several years before, she was taking lessons from me along with six other kids. They had never met a coach like me, hardened by time and falls. These kids needed convincing, and most were riding reschool horses. The young people on that day were difficult. They gave me coltish abuse, cocky in their disregard for my instructions, and making sharp comments. I called them over, formed a line, and looked them up and down, seeing myself in their faces.

Long ago, I had a similar look of belligerence with my own instructor. But he had taught me respect when I saw what his years of riding had taught him. "You're tough?" I asked the kids, as I stood with my weight off my old injured right leg.

"Yeah....Right," came their sharp answer.

"Good," I responded. "Posting trot, no stirrups. I'll be back in thirty minutes." I turned on my heel and walked to the shade of a nearby tree, picked up a Coke and swigged it after raising it to them in a salute.

I wondered, *Who was real in this group?* They looked at one another. No one moved. "Oh, weak, eh?" I said softly from the shade.

That did it. With a sharp glare they turned back to ride the posting trot, the rise and fall to the alternate shoulders of the horse without any leverage from their irons. Horse hoofs made soft thumps in the sand, and leather creaked in the hot sun. After ten minutes the kids started getting weary, their legs wearing out with the effort. They were learning why event riders must be fit with tight leg muscles.

The kids often looked at me as they rode around the arena. First angry, then tired, then pathetic. Passively, I sat and watched. The young people were learning discipline and how to keep going even when it hurt. A good lesson for life, and certainly for eventing, which requires strength, balance, and courage. After about thirty minutes I called them back and we had a quiet lesson. Tired, they listened.

Later Sarah told me that because I had challenged them, this opened her eyes. The kids admitted that their other teachers had been afraid of them. I laughed out loud, and with a burst of strength, swung up on one gelding and jumped their course without stirrups so they would know I was not just talk.

Training a horse is a slow process. Often I am surprised by a rider who does not think his horse feels as he does after a heavy workout. Tired, confused, full of the partnership perhaps, or exhilarated. "Empathy," my father had once said. "Have empathy for the horse." Isn't this what young people need to be taught? To feel their own pain and know they are not alone? To feel another's pain and learn compassion?

Six months later and the training continued. By now Casey had learned to stretch, to reach down with her head and neck, and to relax and lengthen her back muscles. She could hold a frame as she gathered herself back on her haunches, lightened her forehead, arched her neck, and softened her jaw. And finally, Casey had learned to do all of this with the weight of Sarah on her back.

Now it was time to jump. Sarah walked proudly into the sand arena. The mare's dark eyes were smoky and gleaming. They stood in front of the huge oxer I had built, which was a formidable fence, six feet wide and almost five feet high.

Sarah's jump over her mother's car is made in the mind, not really very difficult in itself. But the car was solid and unforgiving if Sarah made a mistake. Sarah had to be able to jump something much bigger than the car to prepare herself mentally. So over the next three months, we worked our way from single small fences of three feet high, to related fences and grids in a line. These exercises taught the horse and rider to communicate what stride to use and what degree of engagement. Both must know how much weight the horse must balance on her quarters to leap the fence.

Six days a week Sarah trained, but practiced jumping only twice a week. She also worked at dressage, the gymnastic flat work to strengthen Casey's haunches. These sessions were forty-five minutes long with an hour's walk afterward. Sarah rode half seat to strengthen her legs. Usually, I sat in the shade with a soda to rest mine.

Afterwards, the mare was cooled out carefully, rubbed down, fed, and returned to the barn. Part of Sarah's training was to ride with no saddle or bridle—a true test of the horse's good will and the rider's preciseness in communicating. Through all of this training Sarah learned commitment to a relationship and to a goal.

During the months of training the bond between them grew like summer grass in the wet northern meadows. Now, as I raised the oxer I gave Sarah my pet coaching phrases: "Don't let the height scare you." "A cow can jump four feet." "Visualize yourself and Casey jumping the fence."

And the trite hard comments used over and over again as well: "No guts, no glory." "No pain no gain." "Ride with the best, die like the rest."

I knew Sarah could do this. Sometimes she searched my face as if looking for herself in my gaze. I recognized that glance and showed her a reflection of confidence. The belief of one person can give another person incredible power, strength for a lifetime. Through Sarah I was passing along the gift my father gave to me.

While Sarah worked, I fed her my philosophies. The rider must choose a horse as a partner or a slave. A partner has a say in the work, in the form the art takes. A slave is forced, but gives nothing away and hides intelligence and genius. A horse either wants to or doesn't. A horse either understands training or doesn't. The teacher of horses must examine her motive. Is it the love of horses? Or is it dominion over them? An artist does not choose slavery. And a horse can understand art.

Sarah wiped her face between jumping. Concentration creased her brow. The bay mare lifted her hooves and touched the dust, then they swept the air, clearing the four-foot oxer. I set the oxer higher. Four feet was nothing for someone who jumps. But when you do this you can feel a sharp pinprick of fear, beating heart, and sweating hands on the reins.

Casey loved to jump. I could see it in the way she drew herself towards the fence, pulled towards it like a planet towards the sun. Casey's hind legs surged under her, her eyes bright and fearless, a meteor coming in with a great spray of sparks. This is what Sarah rode. Over and over I told her, "Thank your mare." I wondered, *Does the mare give to us because Sarah and I have taken so much time to explain the partnership to her?* I think so.

After two-and-a-half months of working over the big oxers, I got a call from Hita, Sarah's mother. She wanted to know if a date had been set. Summer was being pulled into autumn. It was time. Sarah set the date for August 28.

In the midst of all this training, I recalled an incident from my youth. Stoat and Heinburg's truck. Many years before, a man had come to our barn to teach dressage. He was from

Germany and very partial to European warm bloods. A good teacher but pompous.

Pop had been dead for two years. Stoat was learning his trade, eventing, and teaching me as well. One day while I was riding, Heinburg pulled up to the arena in a small pick-up truck. He got out, flipped on a peak cap and swaggered over to us.

"Ah, the little pony!" he said with a sneer of sarcasm. Stoat was an American thoroughbred cross, a little more than sixteen hands high, hardly a pony. I glared, but said nothing.

"Isn't that the pony I saw yesterday?" he continued.

"This is not a pony," I said softly staring down at the man as Stoat restlessly moved his hooves.

The man laughed musically and tipped back his hat. Trying to ignore him I asked Stoat to move on. As we left he shouted to me, "Ah, yes! The pony and the kid I saw galloping yesterday!" Then he laughed again.

Insulting someone is one thing but insulting horses has caused war in the past. Alexander the Great made war to get back his beloved horse, old Bucephalus, whom his enemies had stolen. Heinburg had insulted my horse.

Very well, I thought as I cantered up to the gate and stopped. Stoat quivered as he felt my trembling anger. Being the soldier that he was, he stood quiet. "Open the gate," I quietly, firmly commanded.

With exaggerated mock courtesy, Heinburg swung the gate wide and Stoat and I calmly walked out. In a silky, snide voice, Heinburg threw out one more comment: "You are angry that you ride a pony, eh?"

Beyond Stoat stood Heinburg's truck, shining on the grass. My boss wasn't around, the barn was quiet, it was just Stoat and me in the sun looking at the truck. Birds were singing, my face was hot. I turned and gave the man the look that later I saw burn in the eyes of hunting wolves.

Closing my legs, the gray thoroughbred rose under me, cantering. Like a hawk we flew over the truck, turned, stopped, and stared back at the startled Heinburg. His hands dropped to his sides, motionless, as the gate swung in the breeze.

When I looked at Heinburg with my heart in my eyes and a smoldering spirit, I knew I was a warrior. He knew this, too. Later, alone with Stoat in his box stall, I cried. I could not understand why a person would choose meanness. As an adult, I told myself, *It must be fear. Fear blown into a mind so hard that kindness is forgotten.*

I had told Sarah this story when she was fourteen. That must have been her inspiration for jumping the car. Heinburg would get it twice.

Sarah's day crept upon us like the lion, stalking, hiding under the normal duties of the week. I wondered, *Does Sarah feel its presence?* I do. The feel of the cold chrome of the convertible and the swing of slender, fragile cantering legs. If Sarah and Casey did not clear the car in this rite of passage, death was a possibility, and at the very least, serious injury for both of them. Their safety lay heavily on me.

For years I had competed in cross-country eventing. If the course was difficult I trained and trained, but the edge was belief. What is winning? The best course I ever ran was when Stoat took fifth place. That course was unforgettable. The memory will flash through me completely intact when I die. That was one of those experiences when the world crescendo roared about me and immortality galloped through my veins. This is what Sarah's jump was about. Not about a colored bit of blue ribbon that will fade to gray. The spirit must wear the medals. People will see them in her eyes.

Suddenly the day came, as bright and as clear as childhood. I drove to the sand arena in the woods. Sarah was already there warming up. A slight breeze promised to tickle the mare into excitement. Casey shone like a cathedral. There was power in Casey's gaze as she focused on the ground up ahead. Her legs lightly touched then swept up, flashing black, then russet. Her tail flew behind her like the grace of God.

About ten people, family and friends, stood around. Cameras ready, they waited to witness and to document this rite of passage. Sarah had drawn the people who loved her into this mystery.

Now I was priestess as well as coach. Watching, then silently praying a moment for safety and courage, I lightly pulled out a few strands of my hair. Opening my hand, the breeze took the strands, my give-away, and they floated off to rest on the face of the Mother of us all.

I was left alone. Sarah and Casey cantered around me, the dust hanging in the air. The family did not approach; the moment was wrapped in a shroud. They spoke quietly and glanced around. Slowly, carefully, I built the warm-up fence.

Sarah said nothing. Her hair was tied up under her helmet, but a few golden hairs had crept out and swung around her face. My young Athena. "Jump over this small fence a couple of times," I told her. Sarah's grin was skittish, trembling, and stretching.

Hita drove up with the car, a white boat. Her silver hair free, her face smiling, she drove into the arena and I directed her where to park it. There needed to be a ceremony here, but there was only dust thrown up by black hooves, and a little curling breeze. Looking up I saw a red-tailed hawk. The red eagle, a sacred bird to the people of the Plains. The hawk was big and dark, a woman bird for Sarah. The hawk screamed.

I blocked off the tires to keep the car still, and spread my black cooler over the seats. Then I turned back to Sarah, and raised the fence. Horse hooves pounded with the beating hearts of those waiting to witness. First the canter, canter of the waltz, then a moment of silence as the horse and rider rode on the wind over a fence. They touched the earth and the dance continued. The oxer Sarah and Casey could jump was much bigger than the car. The oxer with its slender poles could fall, but the car could not.

The family crowded together for support. They must have thought that this was insane. As insane as life or as insane as death? We do not choose either one. This is the Mystery I ponder.

Canter, canter...silence...canter, canter. The meditation continued as Sarah and Casey jumped the fence in preparation for the car. Sarah occasionally looked at the car, locking her eyes on the object the way the falcon draws in prey with its gaze.

Hita approached me as I motioned Sarah to let Casey rest. The mother's face was bright but cautious for her daughter as she looked me in the eye and asked, "Can she do this?" The little breeze curled between us.

"Of course," I answered confidently.

The mare walked, fretting. She caught the urgency from Sarah's body and her nimble feet stepped lighter on the ground. Sarah's father, David, walked over. He was a big man dressed the part of an Englishman in a tweed coat and strange green rubber boots. He was nervous. "Uh, Teresa, can Sarah really jump that?" The bay mare looked my way with the light of holy things shining in her eyes.

"Yes, she can," I replied.

Kaj, Hita's best friend, came up next. A practical question: "Where should I stand for the best picture?"

My hand swept north towards the direction where wisdom lies. "That way."

After a brief rest, Sarah picked up Casey's reins and they trotted and cantered. The smell of sage spiraled around me. I had burned it that morning and the sweet scent clung to my wool sweater and reminded me of the hawk. Sarah galloped up to where I stood.

"Are you ready?" I asked, knowing this was the moment.

"Sir! Yes, sir!" Sarah grinned a sideways smile meant to be wicked. I caught her nervousness and gentled it like a frightened mustang.

"Can I really do this, Coach?" Sarah asked, her voice now only sixteen. She was not yet a warrior. I waited, held her gaze for a strong moment. The mare moved in the dust, the breeze lifted her mane.

Softly, I answered, "Of course. Jump the oxer then swing around and jump the car." Sarah took power from me—my power of spirit.

Sarah and Casey swung away. Now there was nothing more for me to do. This was Sarah's leap, her rite of passage.

A cool breeze mingled with the galloping rhythm, the puff, puff, puff of hooves in the sand. All of us float into stillness when time slows in that place of dreams and power.

Sarah's face was pulled down into clear focus. Easily swinging over the fence, they turned, a constellation like Casey's name, Cassiopeia, the Queen of Heaven. They turned around the pole star, my body, positioned as a marker in the ring. The arena was the universe and the particles of sand sent flying by Casey's black hooves were stars.

Sarah and Casey

Sarah and Casey faced life. Life in cold steel harder than flesh and bone, harder than anything but spirit. The mare was a warrior's swift arrow falling towards an elk bull while the family waited at home, cold and hungry.

Four strides, time had stopped. Two strides, pray for bravery— but warriors are brave. One stride, and the horse bunched like the lion and bolted over the white car standing as still and as pale as death.

Sarah's clear voice rang out. She madly galloped back to me, her hand stroking the mare's neck.

"Good girl! Good girl!" I shouted rejoicing in her victory. I stared at Sarah, the bow was now a woman. Her power shone in her face. She would have the strength to face the lion, the Heinburgs of the world. I caressed Casey's soft intelligent face, and leaned close to whisper, "Thank you."

Grasping Sarah's thigh, hard with youth and months of riding, I praised her. "Good girl, Brave!" She beamed at my pride. With a deep sweet breath, I draw her gaze down into mine. The eyes of the falcon met with the eyes of the wolf.

"Now do it again. Never forget." Her face filled with astonishment, then she grinned wickedly. "Sir! Yes, sir!"

Immortality.

Won't Go

This horse won't go. He won't jump.
He's a stubborn one. He's a stupid one, they said.
I looked at that horse standing in the dust.
He looked at me.
I slipped my rope over his head. He nodded his consent.
I said out loud to this horse,
"Hey, this fence is so small
you can jump it from a standstill."
The horse stamped his foot,
so we jumped it from the standstill.
You know? Now that horse is never in that place.
He jumps out.
He's over at my cabin, talking with Grandfather.

Ponokamita, Elkdog

The stallion was silver gray with big white patches and a sprinkling of black spots. A long mane folded carefully in resin draped over an arching neck, and his forelock poured between his eyes. Quarters crouched, head tossed high, he reared half way up.

I first gazed at this magnificent horse when I was seven years old. Mom had taken my brother and me into town to shop. The small dime store stood lazily next to the yellow grocery in the shade of huge hoary oak trees that spread their limbs over the front of both buildings. After food shopping, we wandered into the neighborhood store. On a dusty shelf in the toy section I found the stallion.

The horse's label declared, "Wild Stallion," and the price was $5. Mom bought the toy horse and I clutched him to my chest as we drove home to our white house on the hill. This stallion became my beloved toy, the one who went everywhere with me. I still loved the stallion even when he became scraped and broken.

My brother and I were drawn by the serious children's reality that lives in playthings. For hours I played in the pasture with my toy stallion and my real pony, Babe. Eventually, the toy horse's tail and one lifted foreleg broke off. Mother taped them back on. At some point, somewhere between childhood and adolescence, the stallion disappeared.

Thirty-three years later I saw him again. This time he was running across the Northern Plains of the Blackfeet Reservation.

In my early thirties I visited my first reservation, looking for connections to my Native ancestors, the Osage. The Osage Reservation is in Oklahoma, far from my home in the Pacific Northwest. When I called the Osage Cultural Center, Ruby, a spokesperson, suggested I go to the Blackfeet in Montana as they were Plains people like the Osage.

At the Blackfeet Rez I met Billy, six-feet tall with a chest like a wrestler. He has medium length, raven-wing hair that he always ties back to keep it out of his eyes. He is a passionate, desperate, and idealistic man. In him I see my Native dreams reflected.

I was immediately drawn to Billy because he had a vision to bring back the Native Plains horses for a youth project on the Rez. These horses were the buffalo runners our ancestors rode. The Blackfeet call them *ponokamita,* which means elkdog because they are swift like elk but as gentle as family dogs.

Many Native people want horse programs for their children in order to instill pride and perhaps, to reap some financial gain in a land where jobs are scarce. Billy was able to start such a project at the Blackfeet Reservation. Whenever I talked to Billy on the phone he would tell me with great excitement about the olive dun, or the black roan overo with a mingling of black and white hairs and spotted underside, or the grulla filly whose coat shone an impossible blue. These horses' colors are as varied as patched rock and yellow grass and lodge smoke. When they gather in small herds, the *ponokamita* look like bunches of wildflowers.

Inniskim, a ponokamita

The Plains horses are small and incredibly tough with hooves like stone and a constitution that allows them to live through the harsh winter weather of the Northern Plains. These conditions killed the domesticated American horses who required grain and shoeing. They had lost the instinct that told the wild horses to hide in the gullies when the wind blows and the temperature drops to 40° below. Wild horses know how to paw through the snow for grass and can kill a lion or wolf. Billy had seen one wild stallion chase a young grizzly bear from the horses' range.

In the early part of the twentieth century the United States Cavalry confiscated all of the Plains people's horses. The cavalry feared these horses in the hands of the Natives as much as they feared the Natives with rifles. Most of the horses were slaughtered, but a few were saved and bred by ranchers who saw their worth.

The small Plains horses are thought to have been brought by the Spanish in the seventeenth century. The Spanish still have horses similar to the horses of the Plains. And in North Africa there are the Barb horses, known for their extreme toughness. The Plains horses resemble both of these types.

However, I suspect that the Natives had the horses all along. Elders of various nations have told me that the Plains culture rode horses before the coming of the white man. But then through some tragedy, possibly sickness, many of the horses died out. When Europeans brought horses to North America, the Native people learned to ride easily and quickly. I have often wondered, *Could it be that they already knew the ways of horses?*

Billy has a fossilized horse hoof that the Navajo people gave him. It possibly dates back several thousand years. The path of ice to Siberia links Native America with the nomadic horse culture of Mongolia. Frozen remains of horses have been found in Canada, dated at about seven thousand years old. The horse equipment Native people would have used, a leather bridle, would have decayed rapidly. So there would be little proof of the domestication of the horse in North America.

The Native people of North America had their own breeding programs. They bred different types of horses, such as the war horse, the buffalo horse, and a small draft-type horse. But as the Native nations lost their land and were placed on reservations, these breeding programs were almost lost too.

These wild horses are still with us, with me. When I first saw them thundering across the Northern Plains I recognized some ancient knowing. These horses would carry me closer to my Native home.

After I had been involved with the horse project for a couple of years, Billy gifted me a horse in the old way. The ancestors would not sell a horse but would give him as a gift. In the old days, the gift of a good horse was a gift for life. In the Native culture a great person gives important gifts. You are judged not by what you have, but by what you give away.

When Billy gifted me a *ponokamita,* this was a great honor. This gift made me realize I was being accepted by my friends, and welcomed back into being Native. All I had to do was drive to the rez and catch my gift, a black roan overo paint.

On the Northern Plains the cold breeze warns, *Be careful.* The grass is long and rich for hungry buffalo and horses. This is the land of the circling horizon. On one side of the Plains the spiny backs of the Rockies, and on the other, the long sweep of the Plains stretches into the horizon to finally mingle with the sky.

One day the weather can be warm and the meadow larks singing, and the next, the wind can blow as if trying to carve sculpture from the mountain rocks. I have seen the spring temperature go from 70° one day to 10° below the next. It is a wild place where the great bear, wolves, and horses live on the Plains. This is where I came to collect my gift, Inniskim, which means "Sacred Buffalo Stone" in Blackfeet. This is the stone that the matriarch of the nation uses to call the buffalo to the people in times of hardship.

My friend Hita traveled with me from the Northwest to get the stallion. A good traveling companion, she is big-hearted, brave, and her laughter rings like a bell. Hita is an artist and a wild woman. She is also the mother of my student and adopted daughter, Sarah. Hita is tall and slender, her face always bright and her hair the color of silver-frosted winter grass.

We drove the long, two-day haul across three states and the Rocky Mountains to the Blackfeet Rez in Browning, Montana. The weather for May was warm. As we traveled, the road grew straight and the radio played only country western music and Bible thumping. In typical event-rider fashion, we drove twenty hours without stopping. Junk food and gritty, truck-stop coffee sustained us the entire way.

At the base of the Rockies in Wyoming, we drove through towns now settled by movie stars with extravagant homes, then on over the mountain passes of the spiky peaks with their long hair of lodge pole pine and aspen. Finally, we reached the rolling Great Plains.

Browning sits on the brink of a prairie stretching endlessly in its stark beauty. It has the air of a town on the edge, a mix of strength and poverty, struggle and power. Various religions clash in the bright air of Browning, creating a palatable aura. The townspeople seek something that calls from the mountains and sweeps down to them on the warm Chinook wind. This place holds a timeless dream that fights with the civilization of Western culture.

Billy lives on the Blackfeet Rez with his friend in a beautiful timber house topped with a blue-metal roof. Guests are always welcome. When we arrived, Billy greeted us with open arms, his dark eyes twinkling as he gave both of us a bear hug. Immediately, we were invited to join them for supper.

Afterwards, in the blue dusk of the evening, we went outside to peer through binoculars to catch a glimpse of Inniskim running with the bachelor band. His white patches made it easy to pick him out as he grazed by a lake. Inniskim's hair was a mingling of white and dark, giving a peppered appearance, with big white splashes and a few black spots.

Inniskim was thin from a severe winter on the Plains. Even on my little Pacific Northwest island the madrona trees had exploded from the ice storms. Inniskim had the scars of battle on his back, and his hooves were nearly worn off from outrunning the patriarchs of the Plains, the older stallions who had their family bands.

We watched the little bachelor herd until it was dark and the stars flew out of the blue-black canopy. The Milky Way swirled across the sky and the stars were so bright we could almost hear them ring with light above our heads. We gathered our bed-rolls and walked down to sleep in the lodge. All that night in the tipi I listened for horses through the Plains earth under my head.

The next morning we had coffee and immediately got to work rounding up the wild stallion. First, we coaxed Inniskim down to the heavy-timbered round pen with the lure of food. We also put the tame gelding, Yellow Bird, with him. I had decided that out of respect to Inniskim, I would not take him if he did not want to come. I wanted him to come with me out of friendship, in joy and trust. When he looked at me with his wise, dark, suspicious eyes, I understood, heart to heart, that he mistrusted this whole situation. This was disappointing.

Billy explained the unfortunate first experience Inniskim had with humans. Two cowboys who said they could start young horses had come out to the rez. They roped Inniskim and choked him. Driven by fear and survival, Inniskim jumped a six-and-a-half-foot solid timber fence. Now, when anyone got near, the young stallion thought, *That's enough.* Who could blame him? I was sad about Inniskim's mishandling, and talked to Billy about giving me a younger colt who was untouched. Then I told Inniskim, "This is your choice," and I walked away.

After a few hours, I went down to the corral by myself, shooing away a couple of big men. They politely left so I could speak to Inniskim alone. At first, the stallion looked at me in fear. Horses are honest and I believe they often remember mistreatment for the rest of their lives. I spoke out loud to the wild stallion. "You decide, Inniskim, come or not. If you do, you may help everybody, but if you don't want to, I won't force you." He turned his spotted face and looked at me as if considering my suggestion, then moved off to think.

The sky was turning to a pearly, mussel-shell pink in the West. I left the horses and walked to the house for supper. Guests from different cultures gathered for the intertribal affair. One guest was a journalist from Germany dressed like a character from the Old West. She scared me initially as do all who don't see Native people as human beings first. Such people often don't realize that in the past their own cultures carried the belief of the holiness of the land and the circle of life.

Billy introduced me to a Native woman who was starting some colts and we got into a long pleasant talk about horses that turned into a discussion about prejudice. She asked me if I thought that I looked Indian. My spirit answered before my head. I said to the woman, "I look like a human being."

But every time I go to the rez I am reminded of the long hard road Native people have traveled. The difficult balance of heart, spirit, and mind. The fight between Western civilization and traditional ways. It has been a walk over a raging river spanned by a slender log. It could only be crossed by each generation helping the other generations. My grandpa and I found balance on that slender log by talking about being Native.

What is being Indian and what is not? This is the discussion that is revisited many times. Early on in my own search for my Native roots, I talked to an Osage woman about what would happen if I found out I was not Osage. She laughed and said, "We'd adopt you, Wolf! Like we did a long time ago!"

People are people. Everyone is Native. I believe we travel around a great circle and turn the way the galaxy seems to turn around the pole star. Maybe we come back as people again, but maybe not. As I get older my gut tells me that I will never live in this human form again—that I must not waste my life. But if it is true that I do return from other lives, I do not remember these other turnings. The Mystery must have good reason for hiding them from me.

That night at dinner Billy's friend, Alex, told us a story about the flight of the Nez Perce to Canada and the loss of their horses. Alex told us that the Nez Perce were forced "to come in." As we sat in the living room before a roaring fire, I thought about that term, "come in." *Was this how captivity was described—to bring the Natives into a civilized life?* I wondered. The Native people were already "in," at home on their land. There was hardship being free, being wild, but there had always been hardship. To know the fight is to live!

As Alex spoke, the firelight flashed on his dark face. I marveled at the ancestors' patience and cleverness; at their lodges made of buffalo hide, snug and warm in the storms; and the smoke hole flaps that were designed to pull the smoke away from the lodge. The Old People had to "come in," and they lost almost all of their horses, and their way of life. But now the Nez Perce are breeding their horses again, and some of their people are moving back to their valley, the Willamette, in Oregon.

After dinner and washing up, Hita and I walked down through the wind and blowing snow to the lodge. We started a fire. Hita knelt in front of the blaze as excited as a child. I went out to adjust the smoke flaps so the wind, which was blowing about thirty-five miles per hour, would pull the smoke out of the lodge. Occasionally, snow blew in and landed on Hita's bedroll, but there were no drafts because the liner hung down and covered all holes. Throughout the night the smoke flaps snapped, but I slept soundly, and dreamed of running buffalo. And in my dream I rode on the spotted stallion and I could keep up.

Shining whiteness surrounded the lodge in the morning. The wintery conditions in May made it difficult to get up. Quietly I pulled on my shoes, trying not to wake Hita as I slid through the door flap. As I walked in the blowing snow down to the round pen to see Inniskim, the horses swung their heads around to watch my approach. Yellow Bird and Inniskim were huddled close together for warmth. I grabbed a handful of alfalfa as an offering and Yellow Bird came over immediately.

Inniskim watched as I stroked Yellow Bird. Then slowly he came up to me and I lay my hand on his white-spotted cheek, which was as solid as stone. His eyes turned soft and a look of wonder crossed his face. He knew from my touch and my posture that I would not force him to go with me. In that moment I knew Inniskim would come. Something melted in my heart as I patted the young spotted stallion. Inniskim was mine in a way that I have never owned a horse before. He was a bridge to my ancestors, to our ancestors, who had ridden together.

The snow continued to fall thick and heavy and I was concerned about getting out of the pasture with the truck and horse trailer. I woke Hita and she quickly joined me so we could drive the truck into the prairie pasture, which was covered with snow and turning slick. We backed the rig up to the gate and pulled the bars down to barricade the sides so that the horses could not squeeze through. Then we pulled out the metal divider and put it in the back of the truck.

While Hita and I worked and shivered, Alex walked down to report that with the wind the temperature was about 10° below. First Yellow Bird and then Inniskim walked inside the rig and ate. They were happy to get out of the wind.

After the horses got used to the rig, we shut the doors to see how they would respond. The colts' eyes bulged and we backed down. Frightened, the horses carefully got out of the rig. Yet, they showed no panic and their ears pricked as they listened to my voice. We decided to leave them alone, so we tromped through the blowing snow back to the house.

The hot mug of coffee warmed my chill as I quietly looked at the artwork displayed on shelves and walls. Beaded gauntlets, carved soapstone, a Moari war club, paintings of warriors and horses with their tails tied up for war. There was an image of women standing still, watching a hawk, their hair long and loose or braided neatly. Children and elders looked out of the paintings, a mixture of spring and winter.

Outside the window in the snow stood the Spirit of the War Horse effigy—a horse skull on a post. The skull was gleaming white painted in many colors and adorned with feathers from eagles and red-colored wool. Beyond the war horse, I could see Inniskim standing completely at ease inside the rig, munching his hay. He was ready to leave.

Hita and I slowly walked down, and climbed through the thick logs of the round pen. Softly we shooed Yellow Bird out of the rig and slowly shut the doors with Inniskim inside. There was only one tense moment when Hita couldn't get her door latched, but I held my hands in front of Inniskim, who faced the doors. He stayed in and we latched the door.

The rest of the bachelor band cruised around outside the rig looking for the little stallion. I walked a path to find where the truck wouldn't get stuck in the badger and prairie dog holes. Somehow the horses gallop through this lunar landscape and never take a bad step. In the distance, Billy stood outside his house. His lips were moving but the wind blew his words away as he prayed softly in his Native tongue.

When we got in the truck, I noticed my fingers had white tips, the beginnings of frostbite. We had been outside only a few minutes. As we started to drive out of the pasture, the little bachelor band followed us. Half way up the hill we got stuck, the tires spinning in the slick prairie grass and snow. I was impatient. We needed to be on our way before the mountain pass over the Rockies closed.

Before long Alex walked down the hill dressed in a huge tan carhart, a warm one-piece suit made for working in extreme cold. With his hood pulled down, only his dark eyes showed. "I'm bringing my truck. I'll pull you up the hill."

Shortly after that Billy walked down to the truck and Hita moved over so he could get inside. He turned and gave me a slow look as if to counter my urgency, then spoke: "You see, the Mystery has this in its power too."

"I have faith but horses take time, Billy," I responded.

Wisely, he added, "The Mystery also controls time. You're going to stop and have more coffee first?" He knew we had something else to do before we left the rez.

I nodded and slowly pulled up to the house, the truck and rig lurching and shaking. Surprisingly, Inniskim didn't make a sound. Inside, we warmed up and sipped coffee flavored with hazelnut, which Billy claimed was the choice of all Native people.

After awhile, Alex joined us, and the four of us went back outside and walked over to Billy's workshop where he creates his art. The hut was filled with hides and feathers and horse papers. He searched for a long time through a box of eagle feathers, then pulled out one large one, almost two feet long. "This is Inniskim's feather," he said as he placed the golden feather in my hand.

For practical purposes, Bob then signed Inniskim's ownership papers over to me. He wanted me to have proof of ownership because horse stealing still goes on. I have often wondered, *Can anyone really own a horse with anything, especially paper?* A human did not brand Inniskim, but later I found the thumb print of God on his right shoulder. He also had a big white spot on his left knee, which meant that he was swift.

We took a pinch of cedar, sweet grass, and sage, and put them in a hot frying pan. Then we washed in the smoke with our hands and waved the smoke over our bodies and feet since we were traveling. Bob mixed buffalo fat and red earth paint. As he painted our temples, he prayed in Blackfeet. For me, he prayed, "Have pity on this little one, my little sister, protect her on her journey."

Over Hita, who was older than Bob, he prayed, "Protect this one, my auntie, protect her on her travels." When Bob finished, he looked at us and stated, "Don't take this paint off." We nodded.

As we started off down the road, I had a passing thought of the paint and the Idaho sheriffs who had scrutinized me in the past. Anything was possible as we left the reservation, headed west towards the sea with a real buffalo horse in the rig.

As Hita and I drove up the spine of North America, the snow blew across the windshield. This was skip snow, the kind that says, "We don't want you to leave the reservation." I managed to scratch a hole in the ice in the side window with my pocketknife. Beyond, all I could see was the frozen land.

With a bright smile Hita warmed the situation, joyfully, incredulously declaring, "T, there is a wild stallion in the trailer. We are hauling a wild stallion up this pass in a snowstorm in May." This somehow made Hita happy, the riskiness and strangeness of our trip. When Hita swung her head, her short, silver-blonde hair tossed and I could see the red paint flash across her temples.

The eagle tail feather lay on the dash. When Billy had placed the feather in my hands, Alex had warned, "If the Feds stop you, tell them that it is Inniskim the horse's feather. That will help." I wondered why eagle feathers and ceremonial paint would be threatening to people off the reservation. Here I was, in a country that professed freedom of religion yet hassled Native people for their feathers. I was concerned about this, but I was determined not to hide my Native ways. This time no one would stop us.

The first fifteen miles up the mountain pass were the worst but it was cold enough that the snow blew across the road. There were patches of ice and although I tried to worry, I found that I couldn't. We were protected. I trusted the power of the people and the Mystery who kept me coming to the Blackfeet Reservation. Surprisingly, a white falcon dipped in front of the truck, startling us, her flash of presence a confirmation for my trust.

After two hours of careful driving, we reached the crest of the Rockies and started down. The sun peeked out and the temperature rose. Soon we had the windows down as we cruised along the highway. Inniskim munched hay in the rig as relaxed and as confident with the ride as a seasoned competition horse. We took turns driving for the next twenty hours, determined to reach the dock on Puget Sound before the last ferry departed at two in the morning.

There was plenty of time to think and listen to Emmy Lou Harris sing strong and sweet on the radio. This is the way to travel—close to the ground where I can watch the terrain change. When I drive no one can fool me about what is happening on the land. I can see for myself. If the land is hurting, I see it. I don't like traveling in an airplane at thirty thousand feet, disconnected from the ground with people who don't look at me or speak.

When we reached home it was after two in the morning. I parked the rig at Hita's converted gas station that she had transformed into an art studio. The stallion thumped and rattled in the rig, but I didn't want to unload him in the dark. I slept restlessly for a couple of hours in the front seat. And Hita slept in her sea bed, facing the dark clear water of Puget Sound.

The birds began to sing the sun up, rising like an old grand-father. On that still, gray morning it sounded as if all the birds in the world gathered together to sing. I drove to the little farm where I kept my horses, eager for Inniskim to get out of the rig. The stallion had easily jumped out of the six-foot round pen on the reservation, so I wondered if my fences would hold him. If he decided not to stay, I was too tired to think of trying to catch him. I touched the smooth surface of Inniskim's eagle feather, hoping he would choose to stay.

As I backed the rig to the paddock that would house Inniskim, the feisty Connemara stallion, Sterling Moss, screamed from his stall inside the barn. Inniskim whickered softly his answer. The rest of the horses remained silent. I barricaded the sides of the rig and opened the back of the trailer, unsure what to expect. The stallion stepped out. For a moment, he looked at me. Then Inniskim, Buffalo Stone, quietly walked out on to the grass and into my life. And the ancestors whispered, *The Buffalo will come.*

One year later Inniskim taught dressage to Ocan, one of the Blackfeet students who came from the North Plains to learn what the mixed-blood Osage woman had to teach. They call me *Muckqui Aki,* Wolf Woman. That day I sat on my spotted stallion with my ancestors smiling out of my eyes. Inniskim had called my people to me.

Sun's Own Horse

My life has turned in an unusual way as I approach middle age, falling back into childhood dreams and beauty. When I was a child, the horses spoke with dark eyes and the motions of their bodies. I could understand them more fully. When I became a professional rider I stopped listening to the horses with the innocent clarity of a young person. Finally when I quit riding professionally in my late thirties and slowed down, the horses came swinging back into full voice and I understood them again.

Now in midlife, the horses call on a different part of me, something unusual. It is as if life wished me to ride what my ancestors rode—the horse of the Native Plains. These horses have fallen into my life like fiery stars, and their impact has left me transformed.

Inniskim, Buffalo Stone, was one of these horses; the other one was *Natoowapee Ponokamita*, which means "Sun's Own Horse" in Blackfeet. He was one of the most challenging horses I ever worked with, even more than Belle, the gray mare nicknamed "The Hell Bitch." Sun's Own was certainly more dangerous.

I first laid eyes on Sun's Own while visiting the Blackfeet Reservation with my friend, Pat. We spent four days visiting friends in the area surrounding Browning, Montana. Over dark coffee, wine, fry bread, and hamburgers we talked for hours with friends while children ran in and out, slamming dusty screen doors and playfully shouting. Sometimes the children would sit with us and listen silently while we joked and laughed, told our stories, and solved all the world's problems.

After awhile Pat and I would clamber into the tall red truck with its sleeping pile of cow dogs and we would push on to the next stop. "We're Thelma and Louise on the rez," I told Pat as we drove the dusty backroads. She giggled and tossed her curls—she had just gotten a perm and a divorce.

On our last day we drove up to see the buffalo ponies in a high, wide expanse of land that clung like a mountain goat to the feet of the Rockies. The grass was still stiff with cold and the wind ran like mice through the stalks. The buffalo horses had come to graze and look out over the high vistas. "Look at the new colt!" Pat pointed out excitedly. A small, two-day-old foal with a sweet face and sturdy frame stood close to his mother. The colt was a grulla, the color of a blue steel gun barrel touched with gold. When I was a child, Pop had told me about grulla-colored horses. "These horses are the strongest," Pop explained. "Horses of that color have a thick hide and hard hooves." Since then I have always admired them for their beautiful and unusual color. This colt also had the black primitive stripes on his forelegs, hocks, and ears, hinting of an older ancestry.

The band stallion, Blue, watched us patiently as we admired the horses, but the colt's pitch-black mother laid back her ears and herded her colt away from us and the motionless cow dogs. "Duenna," Pat called out as she watched the independent mare. "No one was ever able to ride Duenna. She's like me!"

We laughed as we clambered back into the truck and the dogs jumped in the back and lay down with deep sighs. We had more friends to visit before heading back to Vashon Island. I soon forgot about the grulla colt.

Three years later a friend from the Blackfeet Reservation, Billy, called me about a troubled horse. Billy had founded a nonprofit group on the rez with the vision of bringing the horses of our ancestors back to the Northern Plains—the swift, sturdy, wise horses of Native America. That morning Billy's voice was broken, tired, and sad as he told me the story of the grulla stallion roped and almost stolen from him. Horses still vanish from the Great Plains of the West, stolen and sold for dog meat down south in California and Texas. The kids in Billy's horse program had witnessed a young man from the rez rope the stallion around the neck and legs and throw him to the ground. The stallion fought in anger as the hard hemp cut into his legs. The children also saw the ropes break and the angry stallion trample his captor. The man was taken to the hospital where he laughed and joked about the stallion not respecting him, unwilling to admit that he had disrespected the horse.

Eventually Billy found the grulla stallion and managed to corral him into a six-foot, timbered round pen. The young stallion was so angry at life, humanity, and captivity that he was violent. No one could get near him without risk of injury. Billy despaired while he contemplated the hard choices that stared at him defiantly in the sparkling eye of the furious stallion.

"Oh god, T, am I going to have to shoot him?" Billy asked.

In an instant I remembered the grulla colt, his soft eyes and tottering legs as he followed tough Duenna, his wild mother.

In a serious, quiet voice he warned, "T, I think he is dangerous! We can't even turn him loose around here where he can get at people. He might kill someone. But I hate to shoot him—he is beautiful, magical."

Softly I responded, "I'll come get him."

I felt a tremendous sadness at the possibility of this horse's life lost through brutality. Besides, there are few of these buffalo horses left in the world. The loss of even one is tragic. They are tough, intelligent, and require time in order to convince them about the partnership with humanity. Buffalo horses are not quite domesticated, but once made a friend, they offer a unique partnership. My first buffalo horse, Inniskim, has shown me this friendship.

Two of my students from Wolftown, Summer and Jamey, went with me two weeks later when I headed for the Blackfeet Rez. Summer was eighteen and Jamey one year younger. They had been working with me since they were twelve and I trusted them around horses without question.

The ominous threat of October weather in the north hung over our driving. Already snow topped the mountains as we rolled along the highways, horse trailer in tow. The radio played cowboy love songs or oldies rock and roll. We would stop for coffee, pop, and candy at the quiet gas stations along the foothills of the Rockies, and then keep driving. We drove over the mountain passes and eased down onto the rolling prairie, and finally to Browning and the rez. We took the only left turn in town and soon arrived at Billy's ranch.

Inside the six-foot timbered pen the young grulla stallion stood with his head lowered and his eyes watchful. His unusual steel blue coat had a black dorsal stripe that swept down his back, with additional stripes that scored his forelegs and hocks. He was barely 14.3 hands high, but he was muscled like a boulder. Wilderness lived in this stallion's eyes under his black forelock.

The most significant feature about this horse was that his ears were flat back, not merely in displeasure but in a kind of fierce hatred. As I stood a good ways back, quietly observing the stallion, one of the young men on the rez casually walked closer to the fence. The stallion bared his teeth and charged the man, lunging furiously over the fence trying to get at him.

At the sight of this burst of anger, Jamey quietly asked, "How are we going to get him into the rig?"

At that moment the stallion made another charge at one of the men standing a little bit closer than we were. This young horse was like a provoked predator with the fierceness of a wolf or a grizzly. His eyes smoldered and he snorted wrath at us.

We all took three steps back. "I don't really know yet," I replied.

Then Summer asked, "How long do you think anyone would last in there?" Without hesitation, I responded, "Seconds…maybe." As I rubbed my forehead I thought, *I am really asking for it this time.*

Billy reassured me the horse was untouched except for the roping incident. He ran the horses in family bands so they were as wild as the buffalo. For a long time I observed the blue stallion, pondering the situation. Every so often I looked at the sky where snow-laden clouds pressed down.

After about two hours of watching the stallion, we barricaded the round pen gate with heavy timber. Then I slowly backed the rig into the pen. The stallion watched with extreme concern, the whites of his eyes showing. His ears stayed flat back, always. We opened up the horse trailer, the divider was already out, and we tied the doors open.

For two days we fed the young stallion in the rig. At first he stayed away, his defiance greater than his hunger. But about four hours later that first afternoon, he began to lip at the hay that had blown down the ramp. Finally, he went half way in. After the first day I watched him go in the rig, grab a mouthful of hay, and then back out quickly. He was beginning to get used to the trailer—the first step in getting him back to Wolftown.

While we waited during those two days, I often rode Lonesome, a bay red roan gelding. I rode him with a war bridle, bareback, galloping across the rolling prairie. I felt as if I could have ridden into the circling horizon forever to join the wild horses. My students, both from Wolftown and the rez, and I watched for hours as the family bands of horses ate and ran and laid down amid the windblown long grass of the Plains. These were days of peace and liberty for me as I waited patiently before taking the next step with the grulla stallion.

At the end of the second day I led Lonesome up to the front of the rig, outside the pen, where the stallion could see him through the trailer windows. The grulla stallion, excited to see this equine friend, surprisingly got into the strange contraption on wheels. I handed Lonesome's lead rope to Summer and then I crawled through the fence line. Softly I crept up to shut the doors while the stallion, still inside, called to Lonesome outside the rig's manger door. My nerves were jittery as I quickly closed the doors before the stallion realized I was there. He was innocent of my trickery.

Immediately the stallion began to kick and scrape the sides of the trailer as he tried to find a way out of this strange box. We left him alone for half an hour. Once he was quiet, we got in the truck and headed back to the Pacific Northwest. As we drove, the stallion was calm whenever we peered through the trailer's window. He just kept watching us with glittering eyes and laid back ears.

Seventeen hours later we pulled up to Wolftown's barn. The next challenge was figuring out how to unload the stallion without getting trampled. First, we barricaded the trailer in the barn aisle and opened a stall door leading into a paddock with a seven-foot-tall fence. I instructed most of my students to stay inside another box stall with the door shut for safety. Then we opened the rig's doors and I stayed behind the doors as the stallion turned and cautiously looked out, sniffing and sizing up his situation. For a moment his ears pricked, then they laid flat again. He moved out of the rig slowly and investigated the aisle way. As we held our breath, he finally went inside the box to see what was in the paddock. My students reached from their box and slid his door shut.

I knew this would be the most difficult horse I had ever worked with. We peered in at him—his eyes still sparked with hatred and his ears still flat back.

A child once told me, "Horses must trust us a great deal—trust that we will bring them food and water. They must trust that we will clean their house and care for them." This child told me if this was done every day at the same time the horse would like it better, and love us for our concern.

When she was done telling me this, I asked her, "Where did you hear that?"

The child answered, "The Fox told the Little Prince that T!"

Billy had named the grulla stallion when we left the rez, "Sun's Own Horse." For the Blackfeet, this is a sacred name because the Sun was God in a way. In time, I gave Sun's Own Horse a nickname, Smoky, after the book, *Smoky,* by Will James.

During those first days, I watched him for hours. He turned his rump to me and his ears never pricked up. I put our other buffalo pony, Inniskim, opposite Smoky in the barn. Perhaps if Smoky saw one of his relatives being handled and loved by people he would begin to trust us. Inniskim sensed the loneliness of the young horse and nickered to him often.

After a week of nothing but anger from the stallion I wondered if this was the right thing to do. I questioned if it was safe for Wolftown. In my entire career, I had never met a horse with this much anger. I called Billy and told him if I decided Sun's Own didn't want to be friends with people then we would have to let him go back to the wild to take his chances. He could not be released on the rez, but so far away from people he might never meet up with humanity again.

Billy responded with a story. There was a Blackfeet warrior, Mountain Horse, and his war stallion fought as fiercely as a grizzly. "He ate people," Billy explained. Then he whispered into the phone, "I think Sun's Own is that horse come back."

After a long pause I replied calmly, "Bill, he is now at my youth project, he cannot eat anyone."

After that, I started feeding Sun's Own by hand. Every day I laid out his food, one handful at a time. He would have to start coming to me or go hungry. Those were long days. He would move up ever so slowly, his heavy muscles sliding under that blue hide, his ears back, watching me with a grim anger.

I am sure that long ago when First Horse came to humanity to become a partner that he or she was treated with kindness. It would be insane to try to force a wild horse to do anything. Now I wondered if domestication was always moral. In the old days the partners of humanity—the horse, dog, cat, and falcon—did not have far to go to return to wilderness and be free of human beings. But some did not choose to leave their human companions. Once when Inniskim got away at Wolftown he stayed near the paddocks, grazing. He did not go visiting my neighbor's racehorse mares. He knew where he should be and waited for us to put him back.

Cookie the falcon flies free at Wolftown and becomes very angry if we lose track of her. Often she will land on my head or arm then peck me as if to scold me for not paying closer attention to her while she flies.

On occasion I ask myself, *How often are our old partners trapped within our worlds and now so domesticated they cannot live wild even if they remotely thought about it?* Perhaps the same is true of humanity.

After four months of patient hand feeding, Smoky came up to me one morning, one step at a time, and lipped hay out of my hand. He breathed a sigh and his ears moved forward. My heart melted as I witnessed his trust returning. After that his eyes softened a bit. He would still move away if I tried to touch him, but he no longer laid his ears back at my approach.

Now started the most risky part of my work with Smoky. I needed to go into the corral with him and put myself within his reach. Some people would have met this stallion's anger with violence, but I was taught if you did that the horse might respect you but never love you. So I took the slow long road to Smoky's heart.

When I first entered the round pen, I expected Smoky to attack me, but he did not. Instead he laid his ears back at my approach and he kicked and reared at me. Alarmed, I ducked out of the way of his black hooves, but I noticed his kicks were pulled at the last moment and the rears carefully timed. He was respecting my space and I realized he was careful not to touch me. I took deep breaths and slowly I began to trust him as he kept a wary eye on me.

In the round paddock the first thing I had to do was establish communication. I knew I could not lounge Smoky yet because of his distrust of ropes. He was free in the round pen and I wanted to be careful not to exhaust him. At first I only asked him to move a step or two, and then I would reward him with a soft word and a brief rest. Then I would ask him to stop, then reward him again. This established who was in charge, a social interaction that happens in every herd of horses. The band is led by the matriarch mare and protected by the band stallion.

Months went by as Smoky and I continued this slow and deliberate dance of trust. In the beginning he would always lay back his ears and kick and rear at me whenever I first entered the round paddock. Eventually he began to ease up on his fierce stance and more easily accept my presence. During those months other rescued horses came and went at Wolftown. Horses came injured and left healed to live with new families, or else they died and were buried at the little farm. Amidst the daily routines of caring for the animals at Wolftown, I always felt the presence of the grulla stallion.

Spring came with its mud and sunshine and strong breezes. Once when going through a gate a strong wind blew the gate shut against me. The stallion was standing close and pressed up tightly against my side in order to avoid the swinging gate. Suddenly, Smoky and I were trapped behind the gate. In that moment my thoughts turned as slowly and as deliberately as stones. *My god, I'm gonna get crushed by a wild horse.... What a stupid thing.* A moment later the little stallion looked at me strangely yet did not step on me or panic. I felt his warm hide and breath and the new found trust between us.

At summer's end, I decided to start the next phase of our training. One day after completing the round pen work with

Smoky, I walked up slowly to him with a soft brush. Instantly his ears swept back. I hesitated. I held the brush out to him and he took a deep breath. On the brush clung the hairs and scent of Inniskim. I waited silently as the slight breeze curled and whispered around us. Smoky stood still and his ears relaxed a bit. I touched him with the brush. Again, his ears swept back and he threw up his head. Then he shifted his front hooves. I reached out again and softly swept his shoulder with the brush. He stood quietly watching me.

In the sunshine I began to brush him and his ears came up and a look of softness seeped into his eyes. His thick hide and mane felt tough and strange almost like a donkey's. After ten months I was grooming and petting Sun's Own softly on the shoulder.

Every day we advanced on where he could be brushed or touched. Smoky was especially sensitive about his head and legs. I could see the scars from the rope burns on his pasterns. I longed to pick up his hard hooves and admire the quality of the horn, which required no shoes.

Undoubtedly Smoky had a long way to go and it was he who defined the rate of our work together. All that winter we worked on voice commands. He learned them easily. One day I was standing in the barn looking at the stallion over the door of his box and he was looking back at me. I told Smoky, "It was you. You were that colt I saw on the rez! How I wish you could have come to me then and been spared all that pain."

Young people come to Wolftown, oftentimes sent by counselors or state workers. They send these inner city kids to Wolftown with the hope that working with animals will help them feel better about themselves and heal some of their emotional wounds. One teen named Malcolm came to Wolftown with long tousled hair that fell into his steel gray eyes. He was a tall young man who always looked down, at first shy and withdrawn. Right away he loved the horses, especially Inniskim and Smoky. For hours Malcolm would watch Smoky and try to entice him to come for a carrot. Malcolm longed for Smoky's trust.

One morning Malcolm arrived at Wolftown with his wool watch cap pulled down low. As he approached me I could see he was limping. He stopped and I took his chin in my right hand and pulled off his cap. His eyes met mine and I saw a look of infinite betrayal and anguish. He had a black eye and a lump on his forehead. One thin tear slid down his cheek. He pulled away roughly and headed for Smoky's paddock. He hung his arms over the paddock door, silent, watching the grulla stallion.

I called his caseworker. "His father beat him while in a drunken rage," she explained. "We've removed him from his home for his own safety." Shocked, I wondered, *What can I do to help Malcolm with his hopelessness and his silent anger and frustration?* Until that day, it had not yet occurred to me the value of the ruined horses of Wolftown. Sun's Own and Malcolm would soon teach me.

I knew Malcolm loved the little grulla stallion so the only thing I could think of was to let him help. When I returned to the barn I handed Malcolm a soft brush. "Come in, let's brush him together." At first Smoky was nervous with Malcolm, perhaps sensing the boy's pain. Slowly, gently, Malcolm began to brush Smoky's steady, steel blue shoulders. Over the next few weeks Malcolm and Smoky became friends. Often I saw the boy smiling and humming softly to the stallion.

One evening after the chores were done the rain began to pelt down. Malcolm and I stood in the trees and watched the horses eat. He had been helping at Wolftown for three months and the trust between us had grown. In a sad and young voice, he asked, "Will Smoky heal? Will he forget? Can we ride him someday?"

As he spoke, I stood very still letting this young man's words sink into me. Malcolm was asking this question about himself as well as the blue stallion.

"If we love and trust and expect good, sometimes miracles happen," I answered softly.

The boy nodded, paused, and then asked, "Why did this happen to Smoky? What did he do to deserve this?"

I swallowed hard before answering. "Nothing, it was bad luck for Smoky to be around people who were cruel. But now he is with kind people. His luck has changed."

The boy smiled slowly.

That second winter I began brushing Smoky softly with the halter and lead rope, gently stroking the soft rope halter along his body as if it were a brush instead of something that would hurt him. This let Smoky get used to the rope halter, and learn to trust what was once pain for him. Now he came when I called him, his eyes softer and filled with wonder. He would stand still when I petted him, and finally, he no longer laid his ears back.

That spring about a year and a half after Smoky first arrived at Wolftown, he learned to be tied. The first time it was to a strong fir tree with a thick heavy rope and I sat with him and talked to him so he wouldn't panic when he felt he could not get loose. I had a big towel and after allowing him to sniff it I stroked his body with it. His head went up in alarm and he pulled back, frightened at this strange thing touching him. The rope broke and he ran off toward his paddock. I quietly put down the towel and went to catch him. I knew this, too, was a test. He might not forgive me for tying him.

Smoky stood snorting in alarm, but he did allow me to catch him and quietly lead him back to the tree. I wrapped a stronger rope around the tree, but this time only holding it instead of tying it. I wanted to give Smoky some room if he pulled back. It was the fear of capture that made this so hard for Smoky.

When he was quiet I started stroking him with the towel. He flew backwards but feeling the rope give a bit he was quieter. He lunged forward and stood still, trembling. I petted him and rewarded him with an apple. Strange things meant pain and danger to the stallion, but he tolerated it from me.

Every day we did this until after about two weeks the towel was nothing to Smoky. Then I added brushing his body with the saddle pad and the little saddle. Both of these new pieces of equipment took a much shorter time, only about four days. He would move away but not bolt off. Soon he just stood still and trusted me.

Young adults sometimes travel internationally to get to Wolftown for an internship and the opportunity to work with the horses and wolves. When Chloe, a new intern from Spain, arrived at Wolftown she instantly fell in love with Smoky. All that summer Chloe helped me get Smoky used to the saddle and girths. Quickly, Smoky began to trust Chloe. I often laughed with amazement as the stallion started to realize that here at Wolftown people were friends. By this time, Smoky had been at Wolftown for nearly three years.

One day the stallion pulled and reared playfully while Chloe was leading him back to his box. He got away from her and ran back to the main gate. Chloe was in tears, thinking the stallion was gone, but Smoky knew where his home was and let me easily catch him.

On a bright cold fall day after Chloe had gone back to Spain I decided it was time to try to sit on Smoky. Malcolm was visiting and it seemed like a good time to take the next step in teaching Smoky trust. I slipped the bitless bridle over Smoky's head. Nothing happened. He just sighed and stood waiting. Silently, Malcolm watched as I saddled Smoky, lounged him, and then sat on his back. Malcolm looked at me longingly.

"When I come back from school will you let me ride him?" Malcolm asked.

"Of course!" I answered.

That day I called Billy and told him that Smoky's days of fear were over. He loved his home here with us and he now had a home forever at Wolftown.

It took three years of working with Smoky to get him to the point of saddle and sitting on him. Through many seasons and many changing moods this horse and this woman ran upstream like salmon with joy, frustration, determination, and finally peace. We are still learning from each other. Today, *Natoowappee Ponokamita,* Sun's Own Horse, is Wolftown's teacher of returning trust and joy in partnership.

Luck of the Irish

The wolves howled in the sanctuary, their melody rolling along with the first light of dawn. This typical Wolftown wake-up call was enough to get my partner and sweetheart Pete out of bed and ready for work. Slowly I opened my eyes and turned to watch Cookie, the Lanner Falcon, perched on her falcon block near the bed. She stared resolutely out the bedroom window as the wolves kept singing.

While the coffee brewed, my malamute dog Kipmik carried Spitty bear, his beloved stuffed toy, around in a lost circle hoping somebody would play. Every morning when I opened the front door, the first face I saw was Sterling, the gray Connamara stallion, looking at me from his little round pen forty feet away. That morning his happy proud face stared with the rapt anticipation of a horse waiting for breakfast to be served.

Two student interns, one from the Blackfeet Reservation and the other from Israel, walked past me on their way to the barn to feed the horses. Pete rushed by, coffee sloshing in his cup, on his way to catch the ferry into Tacoma, a fifteen-minute ride from Vashon Island.

It was another day at Wolftown, and on mornings like this I felt truly blessed. Content, I nestled into my favorite spot, a well-worn, rose-colored chair of impressive design given to me when my great aunt died. She would be astonished to see her stately chair at Wolftown's rustic cabin with big dogs lying next to it and the occasional falcon preening on its armrest.

As I opened the project's mail, I sipped my coffee. There were letters from people who had visited Wolftown, grateful donations in small increments, catalogs of horse equipment, an advertisement for a falcon transmitter, and bills for phone, power, and feed for the birds of prey.

When I finally opened the bank statement, I groaned and stared. The uncaring numbers and words stared back at me. The bottom line truth that day: Wolftown was broke. Every month I did not know how I would pay the bills for the project. I never could save enough money in case of an emergency and what little money I had was gone.

Five years earlier Wolftown had become an official nonprofit organization, and we had hung in there, always on a shoestring budget. From the beginning, the project had been a unique band of animals and people from various places and walks of life who came together to learn and teach something about compassion. We were rich in many things—compassion, empathy, love—but we had always been dollar poor. And on this particular morning it looked as if we had hit rock bottom.

The interns walked by my front window and waved, oblivious to Wolftown's endangered status. I waved back, even attempted a smile as I sat thinking of a way out of our financial dilemma. I had figured our way out of many troubles—problems with permits, food for the animals, a barn for the horses, and even other less pressing money crises, but this was big. There was no money on the horizon—at least that I could see. We were living in the shadow of the country's tragedy of 9/11 and as a nonprofit Wolftown was hit hard as the economy plummeted.

In the past I had bought time by selling off my personal items of value—my saddles, my car, and my little porcelain figurines that I had as a teenager. *Now what?* I wondered. *There is only one thing left that Wolftown has that is worth something.* I opened the front door and peered into the morning. I watched Sterling eat his breakfast. *He is the only thing of value we have left,* I told myself.

Sterling was nine years old and I had owned him since he was eighteen months old. He was my main teaching horse, the one I could always rely on. Most of Wolftown's horses were rescues who few people wanted but Sterling was a prince. If I couldn't raise money Wolftown would not survive.

Sterling was shipped to me on Vashon Island from Connecticut. Both his parents were from Ireland and rather famous for jumping. He was named after the race car driver, Sterling Moss. This horse proved to also be a good jumper, but his dislike of water made it difficult for him to be competitive.

Sterling was the only horse I had ever bought without first seeing him. He was a beautiful sight on his video, running with several colts, holding his head high. He moved with grace and power and had tremendous energy. Sterling showed character as he jumped on the other much bigger colts, trying to dominate them in a playful way. I fell for this horse!

Actually, I didn't buy Sterling. For years I have been a bohemian artist, poet, and writer by profession, and I was broke when I saw the video that Ballywhim Farms sent me. I went to a dear friend of mine and asked him if he would like to help me buy a colt. This friend was also a bohemian artist, but fortunately for him—and me—his father had left him quite a sum of money.

Sterling would be my horse partner and companion. He came to Wolftown as it was forming before the nonprofit status and permits, but we were already doing the work of rescue and teaching compassion. The day he arrived I had been watching a kestrel as he caught birds in the driveway. Since then I have always likened Sterling to that little falcon—quick, proud, smart, and industrious.

From the first day Sterling seemed comfortable at Wolftown and all the kids who helped at the barn loved him. The horse's trustworthiness was quickly apparent after only a few days. One morning a serious twelve-year-old girl, Caitlin, came up to me in the barn and asked in a rather perturbed voice, "T, is it okay for Althea to be underneath the stallion?" Startled by the question, I shook my head *no* as I ran to look over Sterling's door, worried for seven-year-old Althea's safety. I found her sitting between Sterling's hind legs, holding a leg in each hand. Althea looked up at me grinning while Sterling stood rock still, a look of contentment on his face. Once I got Althea out from under Sterling Moss, I proceeded to give the kids a lecture on not using the young stallion as a tent.

I consider Sterling, or "Sterl" as I affectionately call him, the number-one equine teacher at Wolftown. Five days a week Sterling teaches kids to ride, often with no equipment on him. He has taught cross-country jumping and grid work as well as classical riding techniques. This little stallion has changed many kids simply by his quiet good nature. Children who have suffered loss and torment have buried their faces in his mane and hugged him tight, oftentimes when they could not touch another human being.

Sterling has always taken the children's games and antics with good humor and endless patience. Every morning he whickers his greeting when he sees the young people and the kids laugh in return. I quickly realized Sterling was born "trained" as they say, and except for embarrassing me by not getting back into the trailer at the Connamara Testing, and his intense dislike for stepping in water, he has been very easy to work with.

Sterling is not afraid to work hard around Wolftown. I have even pulled firewood with Sterling, tying the logs on to the saddle horn of the western saddle and dragging them behind him. He has gone off island to teach at prison outreach programs and now is in the "Make a Wish Program."

After the beginning of the Iraq war, I began walking Sterling into town instead of driving as a gentle protest against the war and the uses of big oil. It is about a twelve-mile walk and takes about four-and-a-half hours for a round trip. We could go faster if Sterling so desires. With his new rubberized Old Mac boots donated by the Old Mac Company he can trot and canter comfortably on the tarmac. In the process I have gained a new respect for my grandfather who used horses this way for most of his childhood and young adulthood.

The biggest thing I have learned about riding into town with Sterling is that on horseback life slows down to a manageable pace. People stop to talk and visit. The kids wave from school buses, and I can see how the flowers and new buds are doing. For miles I can watch the clouds and think about life uninterrupted. Poetry swirls through me and my muscles stretch. I always get great exercise walking next to the little gray stallion, although he hurries me along if he senses I am tiring.

When I ride him into the small town on Vashon, he calmly puts up with logging trucks and tourists, always the gentle horse. He can walk calmly by backhoes, dump trucks or boats on trailers, and he never even gives them a passing glance. But puddles he views with great distaste and every time we approach one, I can almost hear Sterl mutter in a thick Irish accent, "Aye, ya daft thing! That could be a bog!"

We regularly walk from Wolftown to Thriftway where we pick up donated scrap meat for the wolves. Packing the meat on Sterling's back is an ordeal when the friendly employees at Thriftway load him up in the parking lot next to the grocery store's entrance. Shoppers always find this sight amusing. We tie the bags of meat on the saddle and often I have to walk beside Sterl rather than sit on all that wolf meat. My grandfather told me this about the old days, "You must trust your horse because one big spook and all your groceries and the family could go flying."

At home Sterling and I play at the beautiful meditative art that is classical riding. The sand round pen at the project is surrounded by tall fir trees, situated right next to the extensive wire-fenced wolf enclosures where the wolves watch us with careful curiosity. Sterl and I prefer to work bareback with the bitless bridle. He is a wonderful horse to ride—balanced, intelligent, and very willing to try.

Sterling lives next to our wolf sanctuary where he listens to the howling wolves, tolerant with a careless indifference of these big predators. He even puts up with Cookie the falcon screaming when I carry her while riding Sterling. When a friend of mine from the Buffalo Horse Youth Organization, Billy, first saw Sterling his eyes lit up with joy. Sterling cantered up to him and Billy declared, "Now, this is a horse!" Sterling ended up teaching the subtle art of riding to many of the Blackfeet youth working with the Horse Coalition. They honored the Irish-born Sterling by giving him a Native name, *Estunimottstokey*, which means, "teacher" in Blackfeet.

I thought of all these things about Sterling on that difficult morning as I sat with my decision to offer him for sale in order to save Wolftown. *The only thing I can do is sell this little horse who has been my uncomplaining friend and partner at Wolftown,* I told myself. I knew it was going to really hurt my students. And then I panicked: *This horse was promised that he would never be sold, how would I tell them?*

The sun warmed the land around Wolftown on that long summer day. In the afternoon I made a few phone calls to various horse people around the country. Sterling was quietly well known in some horse circles. Within a day a woman on the East Coast came forward to offer me $25,000. I accepted the offer, and the sale was pending on the veterinary medical check. When I hung up the phone, I cried for the loss of Sterling and for all the other friends in my life I had to sell because I had to pay the bills.

That weekend my students came out to Wolftown to help. They were a diverse little group of children between the ages of twelve and sixteen. They had come to Wolftown for a variety of reasons: Love of horses or animals, counseling, or just a chance to be somewhere compassionate. We all sat in the pasture at Wolftown and I tried to explain the situation. "There is nothing left for me to do but sell Sterling," I told them. "The other horses, no one would want to pay money for them, and the wolves would be killed if Wolftown folded." The children listened seriously and nodded in agreement. Then the youngest said, "Sterl would want you to do this."

Later that day the children rode Sterling. I hardly could bring myself to look at the little gray horse cantering with a happy child holding on to his long thick mane. In that moment he so reminded me of my first pony, Babe, whom I rode throughout my childhood.

The vet check was in three days. If Sterl passed it, and I knew he would, we would have to say good-bye and ship him to Virginia by van. In exchange, Wolftown would be financially secure. I moped around the project and listened to sad, beautiful, poignant music from Ireland, Sterling's homeland.

The following night I got a phone call from a man in California whom I had never met or talked with before.

"My name is John and my mother just passed away from cancer last week," he began slowly, grief thick in his voice.

I was used to people giving Wolftown gifts in memory of someone who had died. Usually a donation of $25, $50, maybe even $200. So, I got a piece of paper to write down the specifics as John continued talking.

"My mother loved animals, you see. And she knew of your project, although she never got a chance to visit. She wrote Wolftown into her will and wanted you to have some funding for whatever you needed it for."

I waited, holding my breath.

"...She willed you twenty-five thousand dollars...."

I gasped, my mind racing. *What are the chances of someone calling and offering the exact sum of Sterling's worth?* I thought to myself in complete disbelief.

John continued, "I am sending it in two payments. Where do I send it?"

After a long silence, John asked, "What's wrong?" Emotions tossed inside me as I explained to him what the project had been going through and what this donation meant.

"Well," John responded at the end of my incredible story, "I guess you won't have to sell Sterl. I guess my mom bought him for Wolftown."

I replied shakily, "Yes, I guess she did."

We finished by giving each other the necessary information. My next phone call was to the buyer in Virginia to tell her the deal was off. "I felt rather bad taking the stallion from a group of children who loved him," she admitted. "So, I am happy for all of you."

"I am happy, too," I replied. "You cannot know how happy I am....I still cannot believe it. I think I am in shock!"

When I told the kids what had happened, they were silent and nodded seriously. Finally, the youngest girl piped up, "I knew it would happen, the entire island was praying that Sterling would stay."

I got a plaque for Sterling's angel, Louise, and hung it by the front gate of Wolftown. Every time I walk by it I thank Louise for her generosity, for Sterling, for me, and for Wolftown.

The Trail Ride

The young girl sat behind me on Sterling Moss' bare back. We rode down the narrow trail, a winding path of deep purple and lavender foxglove. The little gray stallion carried us through the woods decked out in the mature foliage of summertime. Dragonflies, emerald green and blood red, punctuated the mild summer air.

The stallion was quiet and thoughtful as we walked along through the hills that opened into small dark meadows. The afternoon forest was still, the time of day when the deer rest. A bright sun began the slow slide down between the dark trees, silhouetting their branches, making it seem like winter was a long way off.

My twelve-year-old passenger, Serra, called to my dog Kippy, a big malamute, who trailed us. Other than that she was very still. Far away we could hear the chatter and wail of a piliated woodpecker followed by the cry of an osprey as she flew towards the Sound, tending to her young, now half-grown, but not quite ready to leave the nest.

Then Serra asked, "T? What was your favorite moment in your life?"

"Let's see.... My favorite moment in my life?" I sighed and thought along the span of years, looking here and there for moments that might peek out like stars in the night sky.

Finally I answered. "I have more than one. When I was five or six Pop gave me a red bareback pad. That was really a great present. It was a cold Christmas morning and I ran outside and put it on my pony, BB. She was so fuzzy and fat, and her hair stuck out from under that pad.

"Another favorite moment was when I was about seven or eight and my rabbit had babies—I could hear them in the nest."

I kept thinking about those life moments that never fade no matter how much time passes. Sterling's steady sway under us reminded me of long ago and another child and horse.

I turned around smiling, then added, "I think one of my very favorite memories is riding Stoat at Wild Horse. He had been sick and I didn't think we were going to make it to that event, but he got better and the vet thought I could go. It was the best run of my life."

A few more paces down the trail and I recalled perhaps the most magical moment. "But I guess my very favorite memory must be waking up in the wilderness with a wolf sleeping next to me. A wolf I hadn't seen in a very long time."

Serra watched me with considerable seriousness as I shared my favorite memories. She was slight with light brown hair and big dark eyes that reflected maturity and wisdom. Her father was overseas in the Iraq war. He had brought Serra to Wolftown where he volunteered, helping rescued animals. He found compassion and healing for himself and wanted to share it with his daughter.

Serra lived near Tacoma, and despite great adversity, continued to do well in school and help with her four younger brothers and sisters. Sometimes I wondered, *Can I really help these kids who come to Wolftown? Could the simple things the animals teach really make a difference for kids like Serra who face so many difficulties at such a young age?*

Then I asked, "What is the most favorite moment in your life?"

She smiled slightly and answered, "This is. Riding on the trail. I never thought I could ever hope to ride on a horse through the woods."

I returned her shy smile then turned to face our path and watch the trail rise before us.

RESOURCES RECOMMENDED
BY TERESA MARTIN0

WOLFTOWN!

Teresa Martino founded this non-profit organization for wolf, horse, and bird of prey rescue. Martino uses the wisdom and balance of the rescued animals to teach young people compassion and empathy. The work is based on "finding the balance of wilderness." In cooperation with the University of Washington, this intern program teaches wildlife care and stewardship to students from around the world. WOLFTOWN! welcomes members and volunteers.

P.O. Box 13115
Burton, WA 98013
206-463-9113

www.wolftown.org

WILD HORSE AND BURRO FREEDOM ALLIANCE

The WHBFA is a coalition of concerned animal welfare organizations representing over nine million Americans. It works with other groups to protect America's wild horses and burros as an integral part of the U.S. public lands in accordance with the Wild Horse and Burro Act. This excellent site includes the latest news on wild horse and burros issues as well as an educational Kids' Page.

www.savewildhorses.org

THE ALASKA WILDLIFE ALLIANCE

The AWA is the only group in Alaska solely dedicated to the protection of Alaska's wildlife. The organization's mission is the protection of Alaska's natural wildlife for its intrinsic value as well as for the benefit of present and future generations. AWA was founded by Alaskans in 1978 and depends on the grassroots support and activism of members.

P.O. Box 202022
Anchorage, AK 99520
907-277-0897

www.akwildlife.org

GENTLE HORSEMANSHIP

Founded by Chloe B. Rola, this group offers horse training and clinics in the United States, Spain, France, and the United Kingdom. The Gentle Horsemanship website offers information in Spanish, French, and English. Chloe Rola visits Wolftown annually to hold clinics with Teresa Martino.

www.wakanspirit.org

THE AUTHOR

Teresa Tsimmu Martino lives on Vashon Island in the Pacific Northwest where she writes, trains horses, and oversees Wolftown, a nonprofit organization founded by Martino in 1997. This organization is dedicated to the rescue of wolves, horses, and birds of prey as well as mentoring and teaching young people about animals and compassion.

Teresa Martino's other books include *The Wolf, the Woman, the Wilderness: A True Story of Returning Home* (NewSage Press 1997), *Learning from Eagle, Living with Coyote* (Orion Books 1993), and *Coyote Physics* (Wolftown Publishing 1993). The first edition of this book, *Dancer on the Grass,* has been published in English and German (Droemer Knaur 2001).

ABOUT THESE STORIES

The events are true. The places are all fairly accurate as is the time line. The names of the characters in these stories have been changed. Some characters are a composite of several people I have known. A few of my close friends have not had their first names changed. The horses' names are the same except for Belle and Gauguin, who wish to remain anonymous.

OTHER BOOKS BY NEWSAGE PRESS

NewSage Press has published several books related to the human-animal bond. We hope these books will inspire humanity towards a more compassionate and respectful treatment of all living beings.

The Wolf, the Woman, the Wilderness: A True Story of Returning Home
by Teresa Tsimmu Martino

*Polar Dream: The First Solo Expedition by a Woman and
Her Dog to the Magnetic North Pole*
by Helen Thayer, Foreword by Sir Edmund Hillary

Whales: Touching the Mystery
by Doug Thompson

*Blessing the Bridge:
What Animals Teach Us About Death, Dying, and Beyond*
by Rita M. Reynolds

Three Cats, Two Dogs, One Journey Through Multiple Pet Loss
by David Congalton
Award Winner, Merial Human-Animal Bond, Best Book, 2000

*Conversations with Animals: Cherished Messages and Memories
as Told by an Animal Communicator*
by Lydia Hiby with Bonnie Weintraub

Unforgettable Mutts: Pure of Heart Not of Breed
by Karen Derrico

Food Pets Die For: Shocking Facts About Pet Food
by Ann N. Martin

Protect Your Pet: More Shocking Facts
by Ann N. Martin

Pets at Risk: From Allergies to Cancer, Remedies for an Unsuspected Epidemic
by Alfred J. Plechner, D.V.M. *with* Martin Zucker

When Your Pet Outlives You: Protecting Animal Companions After You Die
by David Congalton & Charlotte Alexander
Award Winner, CWA Muse Medallion 2002

NewSage Press
PO Box 607, Troutdale, OR 97060-0607

Phone Toll Free 877-695-2211; Fax 503-695-5406
Email: info@newsagepress.com

Distributed to bookstores by Publishers Group West
800-788-3123, PGW Canada 800-463-3981